Practical Guide to the Operational Use of the MK19 Grenade Launcher

By Erik Lawrence

Copyright ©2014 Erik Lawrence

All rights reserved. No part of this book may be reproduced or transmitted in any form or by any means, electronic or mechanical, including photocopying, recording, or by an information storage and retrieval system without permission in writing from the publisher. Exceptions to this include reviewers who may quote brief passages in a review to be printed in a magazine, newspaper, or on the Internet. For information, please contact:

Erik Lawrence
www.vig-sec.com   erik@vig-sec.com

Although the author and publisher have made every effort to ensure the accuracy and completeness of information contained in this book, we assume no responsibility for the use or misuse of information contained in this book, errors, inaccuracies, omissions, or any inconsistency herein. Portions of this manual are excerpts from outside sources but have been validated and modified as necessary.

Printed and bound in the United States of America

First printing 2008
Second Printing 2014

ISBN-10: 1-941998-12-7
ISBN-13: 978-1-941998-12-0
EBOOK – ISBN-13: 978-1-941998-31-1

LCCN: Not yet assigned

ATTENTION US MILITARY UNITS, US GOVERNMENT AGENCIES AND PROFESSIONAL ORGANIZATIONS: Quantity discounts are available on bulk purchases of this book. Special books or book excerpts can also be created to fit specific needs. For information, please contact:

Erik Lawrence
www.vig-sec.com   erik@vig-sec.com

Firearms are potentially dangerous and must be handled responsibly by individuals. The technical information presented in this manual reflects the author's research, beliefs, and experiences. The information in this book is presented for academic study only. Neither the author nor the publisher assumes any responsibility for the use or misuse of information contained in this book.

SAFETY NOTICE
Before starting an inspection, ensure the weapon is cleared. Do not manipulate the trigger until the weapon has been cleared of all ammunition. Inspect the chamber to ensure that it is empty and no ammunition is present. Keep the weapon oriented in a safe direction when loading and handling.

AMMUNITION NOTICE- These weapons fire multiple types of grenades, and they must come from trusted sources; never fire captured grenades. Know the capabilities and limitation of each type of grenade. The 40mm grenades used in the MK19 grenade launcher (40 x 53mm) are not the same as in the M203 (40 x 46mm), which are fired at a lower velocity. Firing the incorrect ammunition will damage the weapon and possibly injure the operator/assistant operator.

Training should be received from knowledgeable and experienced operators on this particular weapons system. Vigilant Security Services, LLC Training provides this training and continually perfects its instruction with up-to-date information from actual use.

www.vig-sec.com

PREFACE

This manual is intended to be a reference for those involved in the use, maintenance and instruction of the featured firearm. My aim in writing these manuals is to set the record straight and dispel many of the false assumptions related to the different firearms. The early sections of the manual contain background material on the featured firearm which allows the user to gain the basic building blocks for further education. The firearms featured in these manuals have been used for decades by our allies and enemies, and will be for the foreseeable future, so why are we not experts with them? If I am fighting with the firearm or providing instruction on a firearm, I want to use and know their system better than they do.

The rationale for writing these manuals comes from the fact that there are not libraries of easily accessible references to use in developing your own training system for these firearms. Many of the old military field manuals are decades old and were incorrectly translated by someone who had no idea what the firearm could do, let alone basic firearm knowledge. We started from the ground up and developed the manuals to provide instruction in progressive steps that could be easily grasped and continually referred back to. A good grounding in the basics of firearms, safety, and instruction allows the user to use these manuals to their maximum value. A competent user will find little difficulty in interpreting and applying the information in the manual to their own training program.

The guide goes through the most fundamental parts of the firearm in detail and more advanced techniques are not covered as extensively. With this in mind the user can use these principles and adapt it as needed to their required level of instruction. The emphasis of this guide is in acquiring familiarity with the fundamentals of all firearms and learned competence rather than becoming a firearms guru.

Many of the points in these guides were developed from scratch in theatres of conflict and are continually improved and updated for each edition. I have continually used vetted points from users and professionals in the guides to continually update them to the best known practices for each particular firearm. If it is valid and relevant we will include it in the next edition.

Please note that this guide assumes some familiarity with the basic concepts in firearm safety, gun handling skills, common sense and an ability to process new information. Readers should have knowledge of the difference in calibers, countries of origin, and the knowledge of the priority of the skills needed for development.

I hope you find this work useful and remember that a manual does not replace proper training and hands on experience. Please email comments to erik@vig-sec.com, particularly if you find any errors or glaring omissions.

Erik Lawrence

Table of Contents

Section 1 1

  Introduction 1

    Description.. 1

    Background.. 4

    Variants 5

Section 2 8

  Maintenance.. 8

    Weapons Conditions.. 8

    Clearing the MK19 in Condition 1 8

    Clearing the MK19 in Condition 4 12

    Disassembling the MK19 13

    Cleaning, Lubrication, and Preventive Maintenance for the MK19 27

    Assembling the MK19.. 30

    Function Check Procedures... 35

Section 3... 36

  Operation and Function... 36

    Cycle of Operation 41

    Operations Checklist... 44

    Ground and Vehicle Mounts 46

    Loading the MK19... 63

    Firing the MK19 66

Section 4 70

  Performance Problems.. 70

    Stoppages, Malfunctions, Immediate Actions, and Remedial Actions 70

Appendix A - Ammunition.. 80

MK19 MOD3
Grenade Machine Gun

Section 1

Introduction

The objective of this manual is to allow the reader to be able to use the MK19, Mod 3 Automatic Grenade Launcher competently. The manual will give the reader background/specifications of the weapon, instructions on its operation, disassembly and assembly; proper firing procedure; and malfunction/misfire procedures. Operator level maintenance will also be detailed to allow the reader to understand and become competent in the use and maintenance of the MK19, Mod 3 Grenade Launcher.

Description

The MK19 is an air-cooled, blowback-operated machine gun with five major assemblies. A disintegrating metallic link belt feeds ammunition through the left side of the weapon.

The MK19 supports the soldier in both the offense and defense. It gives the unit the capability of laying down a heavy volume of close, accurate, and continuous fire. The MK19 can also:
- Protect motor movements, assembly areas, and in a bivouac.
- Defend against hovering rotary aircraft.
- Destroy lightly armored vehicles.
- Fire on suspected enemy positions.
- Provide high volumes of fire into an engagement area (EA).
- Cover obstacles.
- Provide indirect fire from defilade positions.

Figure 1-1 MK19 Mod 3

MK19 TECHNICAL DATA

MK19 (MOD 3):
Weight without feed throat	77.6 pounds
Weight with feed throat	78.0 pounds
Length	43.1 inches
Width	14.0 inches
Height	8.8 inches

MK 64 (MOD 7) gun cradle:
Weight	21.0 pounds
Length	17.5 inches
Height	9.5 inches

Tripod (M3) weight: 44.00 pounds

Gun and cradle: Weight without feed throat - 98.6 pounds
Weight with feed throat - 99.0 pounds

Gun, cradle, and tripod: Weight without feed throat - 142.6 pounds
Weight with feed throat - 143.0 pounds

Ammunition: M430 (HEDP)
M383 (HE)
M918 (TP)
M922 (DUMMY)

Mounts:
M3 tripod
M4 pedestal
M66 ring M918 (TP)
HMMWV weapon platform M922 (dummy)
M113 APC commander's cupola
MK 46
MK 93 Hydraulic

NOTE: Keep the feed throat attached to the weapon.

MK19 OPERATIONAL DATA

Maximum range:	2,212 meters
Maximum effective range:	1,500 meters (point target) 2,212 meters (area target)
Rates of fire:	Sustained 40 rounds per minute Rapid 60 rounds per minute Cyclic 325 to 375 rounds per minute
Ammunition:	M430 HEDP 2-inch armor & 15-meter casualty radius M383 HE 15-meter casualty radius
Service frequency:	50,000 rounds
Elevation, tripod controlled:	100 mils
Depression, tripod controlled:	258 mils
Traverse, tripod controlled:	800 mils (400 left plus 400 right)
Muzzle velocity (average):	798 feet per second
Recoil forces (average):	500 pounds
Angle of automatic fire:	0 to 70 degrees elevation (automatic fire), based on mounting arrangements
Ammunition Weights:	48 rounds in M548 metal container - 62 pounds 32 rounds in PA120 metal container - 42 pounds

Background

Although the MK19 is a recent entry into the Army's inventory, development began in 1963. The first version was a hand-cranked, multiple-grenade launcher called the MK 18. In 1966, the need for more firepower inspired the development of a self-powered 40mm machine gun called the MK19, MOD 0. This model was neither reliable nor safe enough for use as a military weapon system. Product improvements begun in 1971 resulted in the 1972 MOD 1, of which only six were produced. The MOD 1 performed effectively in Navy riverine patrol craft, and broader applications for the MK19 were found. In 1973, the Navy developed the MOD 2, which featured improved reliability, safety, and maintainability. In 1976, a complete redesign resulted in the MK19, MOD 3, which the Army adopted in 1983. The Army now uses the MK19 within the tactical environment for defense, retrograde, patrolling, rear area security, urban operations, and special operations.

Figure 1-2 Early MK19 Mod 2 on riverine patrol in Vietnam

Variants

HK GMG: GRENADE MACHINE GUN

Figure 1-3 HK GMG

Caliber: 40 x 53mm High-velocity Grenade
Length: 46.5 inches/1180mm
Width: 8.9 inches/226mm
Height: 11inches/280mm
Weight unloaded: 62 pounds/29 Kg
Barrel length: 8.9 inches/226mm

The HK Grenade Machine Gun is presently being fielded with select U.S. Special Operations units, replacing the U.S. MK19 GMG. The HK GMG is available from series production at a unit cost well below the purchase cost of the MK19.

Its advanced features, excellent accuracy, operator-convertible feed direction and removable barrel, night-fighting capability with NVGs, and unmatched operator safety features are all unique hallmarks of the HK GMG.

The GMG uses an aluminum receiver for reduced weight and manufacturing costs. Other features include a fluted chamber for equal pressure on the cartridge case and positive extraction and ejection, advanced primer ignition, and a barrel that is easily removable for field stripping, with the use of tools. This feature is also an advantage in the event that a high-explosive projectile becomes lodged in the bore.

The bolt reciprocates on a massive guide rod and is stabilized by two steel rails, all of which are bolted to the receiver, eliminating the need for welding in the receiver.

The gun mounts on the standard U.S. tripod, on various vehicle mounts, or on an aluminum multi-purpose tripod that provides assorted high-slow firing positions. An adjustable stabilizing shoulder rod is mounted to the receiver for additional controllability during free gun firing.

Clearing the gun consists of simply lifting the feed tray cover and removing the belt. The position of the ambidextrous charging handle allows the shooter to cock and clear the gun without reaching near the ammunition belt and feed way.

Both the gun and the tripod can be easily transported in a "backpack" configuration by a two-man team.

AGS-17

Figure 1-4 AGS-17

Designation: ASG-17 "Plamya" (Flame)
Type: Automatic Grenade Launcher
Country of origin: Soviet Union
Operation: Belt-fed Automatic Action
Caliber: 30mm
Service year: 1975
Overall length: 33 inches/840 mm
Weight (loaded): 39.6 pounds/18 kg
Rate of fire: 65 rounds per minute
Rounds: 29 round belt magazine
Range: 1600 meters

The ASG-17 "Plamya" (Flame) is a belt-fed automatic action, automatic grenade launcher produced by NA. It is chambered to fire 30 mm ammunition and was first produced in 1975.

The AGS-17 is a heavy infantry support weapon designed to operate from a tripod or mounted on an installation or vehicle. The AGS-17 fires a steady rate of 30mm grenades in either direct or indirect fire modes to provide suppressive and lethal fire support against soft-skinned targets or fortifications targets.

The weapon operates using a blowback mechanism to sustain operation. Rounds are fired through a rifled barrel, which is removable quickly to reduce barrel stress.

Ammunition is held in a metal box feed and is linked. Standard boxes contain 29 rounds of linked ammunition.

The tripod is equipped with fine-leveling equipment for indirect fire trajectories.

Section 2

Maintenance

Safety Rules- The following safety rules apply at all times to all weapons.

1. Treat every weapon as if it were loaded.
2. Never point a weapon at anything you do not intend to shoot.
3. Keep your finger straight and off the trigger until you are ready to fire.
4. Keep the weapon on "SAFE" until you are ready to fire.

Weapons Conditions

A. <u>Condition 1</u>: Ammunition is in the position on the feed tray with the cover closed. The weapon has been charged twice. The bolt is locked to the rear and the safety is on **SAFE**.

B. <u>Condition 2</u>: This weapon condition does not apply to the MK19.

C. <u>Condition 3</u>: Ammunition is in the position on the feed tray with the cover closed. The weapon has been charged once. The chamber is empty. The bolt is forward and the safety is on **SAFE**.

D. <u>Condition 4</u>: The feed tray is clear of ammunition, the chamber is empty, the bolt is forward, and the safety is on **SAFE**.

Clearing the MK19 in Condition 1

The MK19 is cleared differently in a firing situation than in a non-firing situation.

Firing Situation. In a firing situation, use the following procedures to clear the MK19:

(1) Move the safety switch to S (SAFE) (Figure 2-1).

Practical Guide to the Operational Use of the **MK19 MOD3 Grenade Machine Gun**

Figure 2-1 S (SAFE) position

(2) Open the top cover assembly (Figure 2-2) by rotating the feed tray cover latch and lifting the feed tray forward. If all the ammunition has NOT been fired, the bolt is to the rear, and a round is on the bolt face. If the bolt is forward, lock it to the rear.

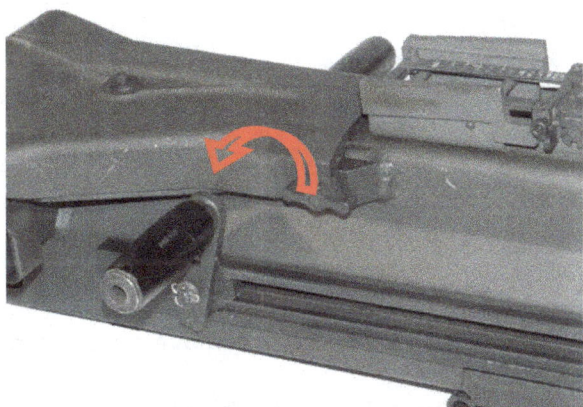

Figure 2-2 Opening the top cover assembly

(3) Take the ammunition from the feed tray by reaching beneath the feed tray and pressing the primary and secondary positioning pawls. While pressing the position pawls, slide the linked rounds out of the MK19 through the feed throat (Figure 2-3a).

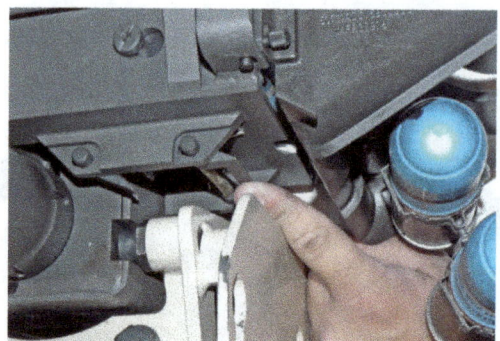

Figure 2-3a Removal of linked rounds from feeder

(4) Insert a section of the cleaning rod or bayonet through either side of the receiver rail. Place it on top of the live round or cartridge case, as close to the bolt face as possible, and push down (Figure 2-3b). This action forces the round out of the MK19.

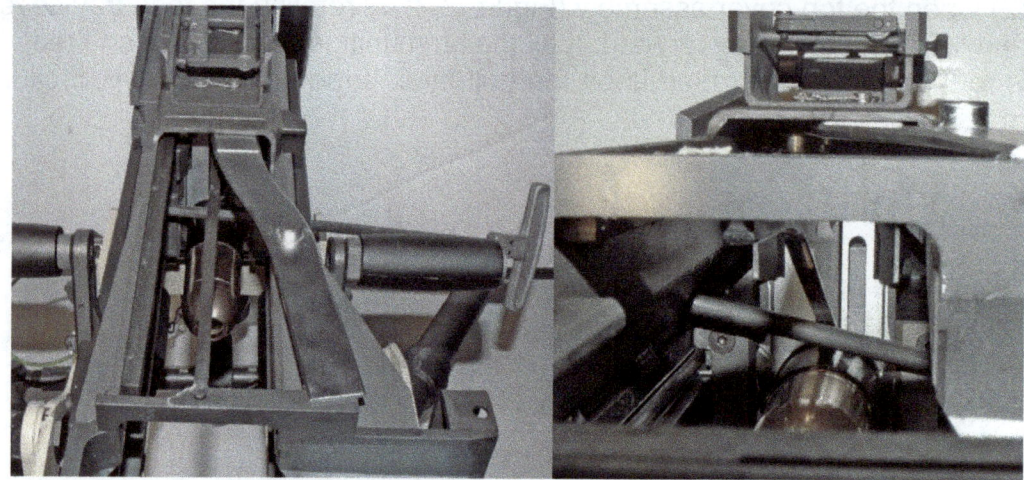

Top view   **Front view**
Figure 2-3b Use of a cleaning rod to remove round from bolt face

(5) Lower (1) the charging handles on both sides by pressing in the lock to rotate (2) the handles down, and then pull (3) both charger handles to the rear (Figure 2-4).

Figure 2-4 Charger handles

(6) Inspect the chamber and bolt face to ensure that no live rounds are in the weapon.

(7) Place the safety switch on F (FIRE) (Figure 2-5).

Figure 2-5 Safety in FIRE position

(8) <u>Maintain rearward pressure on the charging handle</u>, press the trigger and ease the bolt forward (Figure 2-6).

Figure 2-6 Pressing the trigger to release the bolt

(9) Place the safety switch on S (SAFE) (Figure 2-7).

Figure 2-7 S (SAFE) position

Clearing the MK19 in Condition 4

Non-firing Situation. In a non-firing situation, use the following procedures to clear the MK19:
    (1) Place the safety switch on S (SAFE).
    (2) Open the top cover assembly.
    (3) Lower one or both charger handles.
    (4) Pull the charger handle slightly to the rear.
    (5) Allow sufficient space between the face of the bolt and the chamber to see both.
    (6) Check for live ammunition.
    (7) Ride the bolt forward.
    (8) Return the charger handle to its original upright position.

Disassembling the MK19

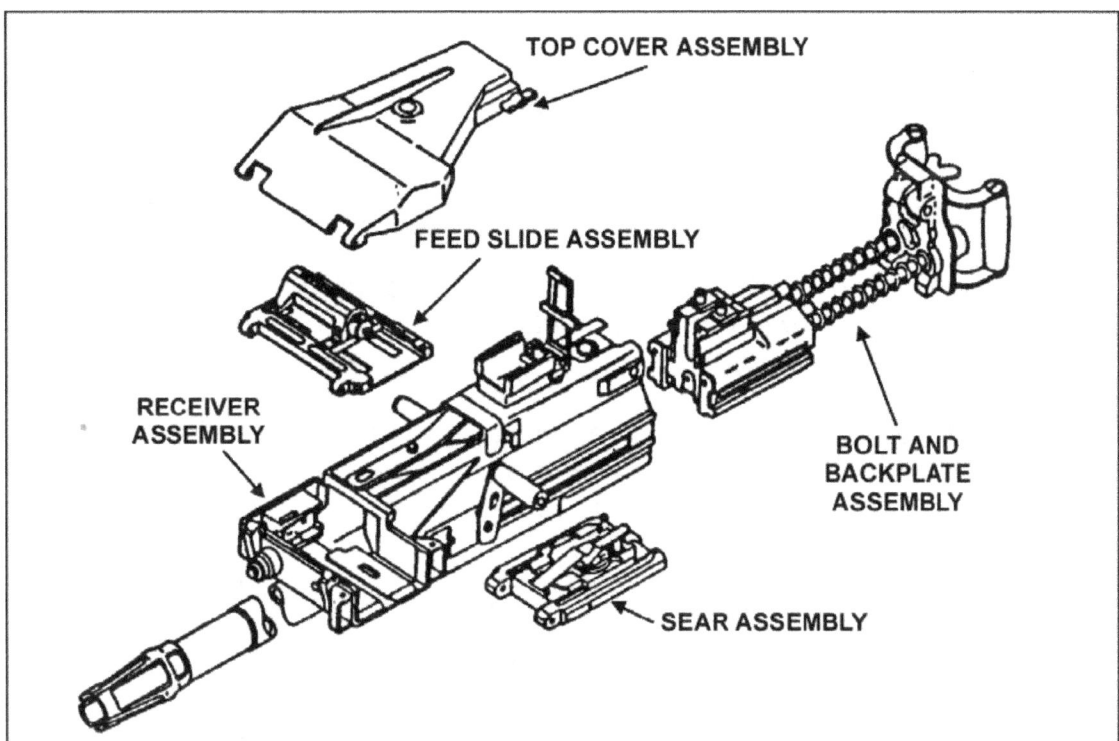

Figure 2-8 MK19 Mod 3 Sub Assemblies

MK19 Mod 3 Sub Assemblies

A. **Receiver Assembly.** Holds the barrel and other parts of the gun. Ammunition is fed into the left side of the receiver through the feed-throat assembly. The MK19's barrel will not overheat, even after prolonged firing.

B. **Feed Slide Assembly and Tray.** Holds the rounds in the feeder and indexes the ammunition into position for delinking.

C. **Top Cover Assembly.** Holds the feed slide assembly and tray. It is opened by a latch (left side) for loading or to clean and inspect feeder area. A blade-type front sight is attached to the top cover assembly (Figure 2-9).

D. **Sear Assembly.** Holds the receiver sear. Trigger action releases the sear and allows the bolt to go forward. The safety is attached to the sear assembly.

E. **Bolt and Backplate Assembly.** The bolt fires the round when the sear is depressed by trigger action. The recoil springs drive the bolt forward on the receiver rails. The guide rods hold the springs in position. Trigger and handgrips are located on the backplate assembly.

F. **Feed Throat Assembly.** Allows smooth feeding of 40mm ammunition. It attaches to the forward left side of the receiver by two sets of spring-loaded retaining pins. Without a feed throat, machine gun stoppages may occur because of twisted or misaligned rounds.

G. **Leaf-Type Rear Sight (with adjustable range plate).** Is marked in 100-meter intervals from 300 to 1,500 meters. The sight is mounted on a spring dovetail base to the receiver assembly (Figure 2-10). Before moving the weapon, the gunner folds the sight forward to a horizontal position. The rear sight can be adjusted for range and windage.

(1) *Range.* Different adjustments can be made to the range. Use the rear- sight slide release to make *major adjustments* to the range. Use the elevation wheel to make *fine adjustments* to the range.

(2) *Windage.* Use the rear sight to adjust for windage. One click equals a 1-mil change. To move the sight to the *right*, turn the windage screw clockwise. To move the sight to the *left*, turn the windage screw counterclockwise.

Figure 2-9 Front sight on top cover assembly

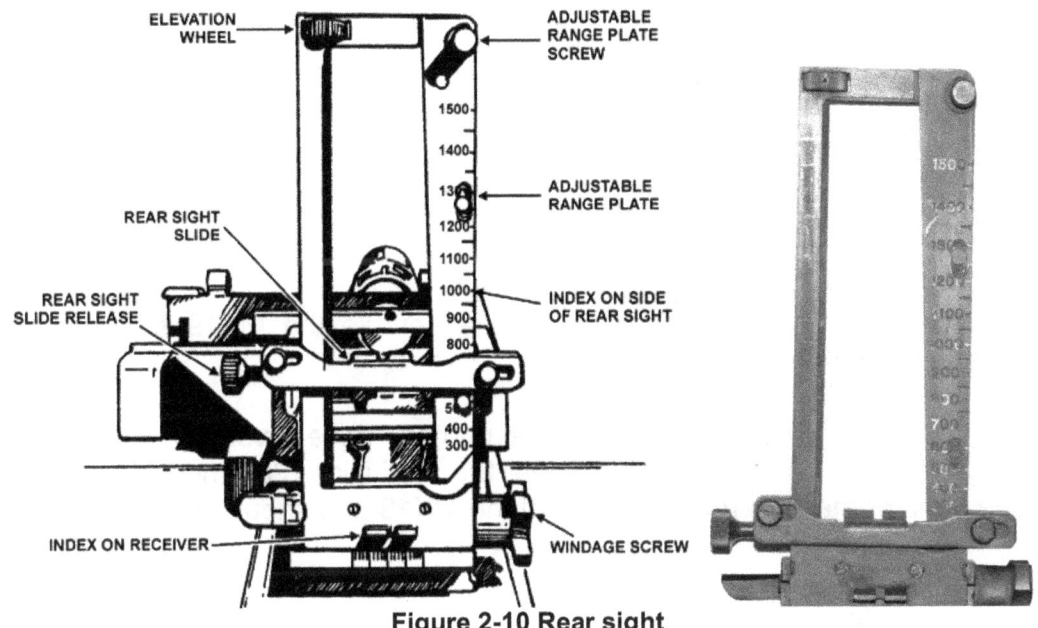

Figure 2-10 Rear sight

Disassembly

NOTE- Place the grenade launcher's parts on a flat, clean surface with the muzzle oriented in a safe direction.

When the operator begins to disassemble the grenade launcher, it should be done in the following order:

Only qualified ordnance personnel should disassemble the MK19 beyond the steps detailed in this section.

High-friction areas — The underside of the primary drive lever (3), the vertical cam assembly (4), the bolt (8), and the area where the feed slide (20) and feed slide tray (19) touch have been treated to prolong the life of the MK19 and should be — during cleaning and handling.

Disassembly includes removal of parts to the extent explained in this section. To ensure that parts are not lost and are replaced properly, place them (in the order they are taken off) on a clean flat surface. A spent cartridge casing, a section of cleaning rod, and a cartridge link may be used as removal and replacement tools.

A. To disassemble:

(1) Clear the weapon as described previously.

(2) Take out the secondary drive lever by following these procedures:

CAUTION- The sear assembly should be removed only in a clean and well-lit area because a small pin could possibly fall out and become lost, which makes the gun inoperable.

> (a) Raise the top cover assembly and push the secondary drive lever pivot post from the outside of the top cover assembly. Some modified MK19s have this post screwed to the top cover; if so, remove the screw and washer to remove the secondary drive lever.

> (b) Separate the secondary drive lever from the top cover assembly (1) then pull it from the top cover (2) (Figure 2-11).

> (c) Tap lightly on the secondary lever pivot post with any available tool, if necessary.

Figure 2-11 Secondary drive lever removal

(d) Take the secondary drive lever from the slide assembly, and allow the feed slide and tray assembly to close.

(3) Take off the top cover assembly by following these procedures:

(a) Hold the top cover straight up with one hand.

(b) Pull the top cover pins from both sides (Figure 2-12).

(c) Lift the top cover assembly straight up and off.

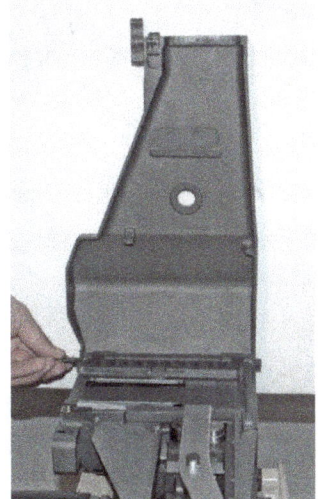

Figure 2-12 Top cover assembly

(4) Take out the feed slide assembly and separate the feed slide from the feed tray by following these procedures:

(a) Align the tabs on the feed slide with the slots in the feed tray and lift the feed slide straight up (Figure 2-13).

Figure 2-13 Feed slide assembly

(b) Take out the feed tray by lifting it straight up from the receiver (Figure 2-14).

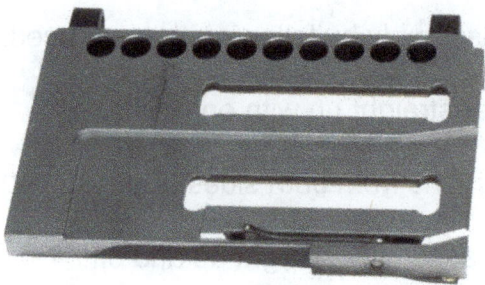

Figure 2-14 Feed tray

(5) Take off the alignment guide by following these procedures:

(a) Depress the tip of the alignment guide spring with the secondary drive lever or a cleaning rod section.

(b) Slide the alignment guide out of the receiver by pulling the assembly slightly rearward (Figure 2-15a and 21-5b).

Figure 2-15a   **Figure 2-15b**
Alignment guide removal

(6) Take out the ogive plunger by pulling it out through the inside wall of the receiver (Figures 2-16a & b).

Figure 2-16a   **Figure 2-16b**
Ogive plunger removal

(7) Take off the round-positioning block by following these procedures:

    (a) Push the round-positioning block into the right side of the gun.

    (b) Slide the round-positioning block forward.

    (c) Release the round-positioning block forward from the keyslots in the receiver wall and pull the block out to the left (Figures 2-17a-c).

*Practical Guide to the Operational Use of the **MK19 MOD3 Grenade Machine Gun***

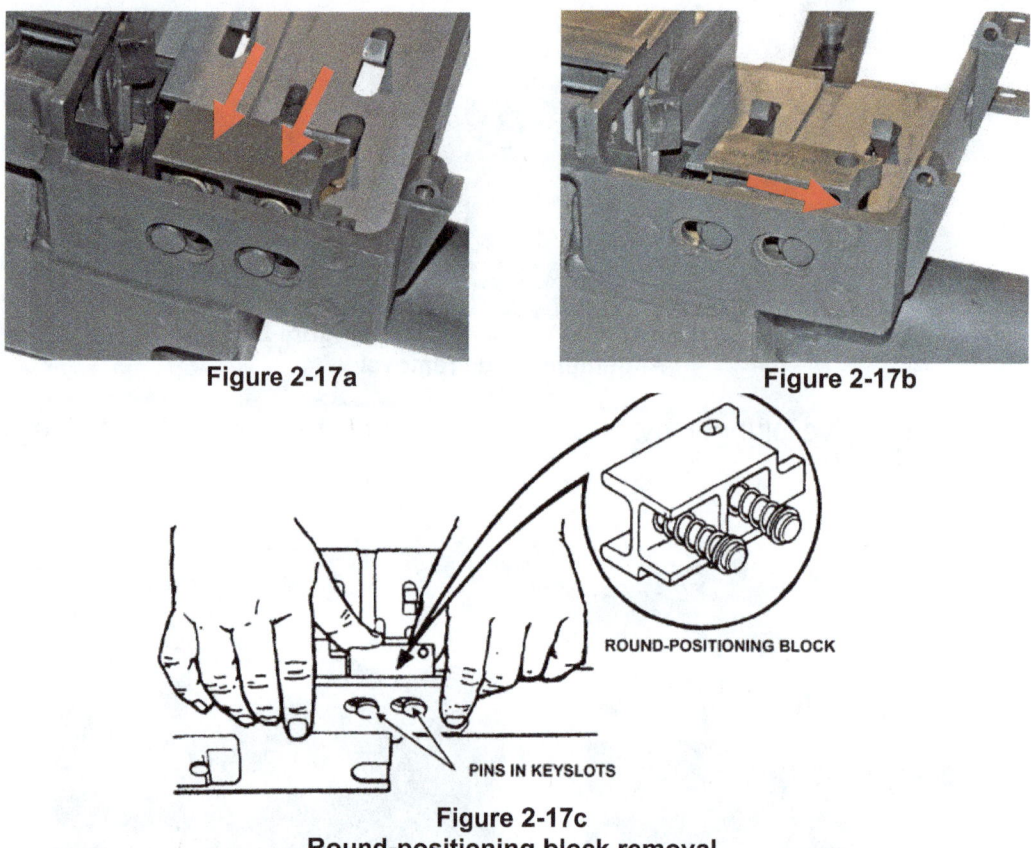

Figure 2-17a   Figure 2-17b

Figure 2-17c
Round-positioning block removal

(8) Take out the bolt and backplate assembly by following these procedures:

    (a) Place the safety switch in the F (FIRE) position.

    (b) Pull out the backplate pin using the rim of a spent cartridge case or metal link.

    (c) Pry outward on the pin lip and remove the pin with the fingers (Figure 2-18). If the pin cannot be removed with the fingers, lightly hit the small end of the pin with the secondary drive lever until the pin comes loose.

Figure 2-18 Backplate pin

(d) Grasp the control grips with both hands and lift up slightly to disengage the backplate from the locking lugs in the receiver.

(e) Pull the bolt and backplate assembly to the rear.

(f) Once the bolt clears the sear, catch the bolt in one hand to prevent damage to the backplate assembly (Figure 2-19a & 2-19b).

WARNING- The backplate is under extreme pressure when the bolt is in the rear position. To avoid serious injury, ensure the bolt is forward before removing the backplate pin.

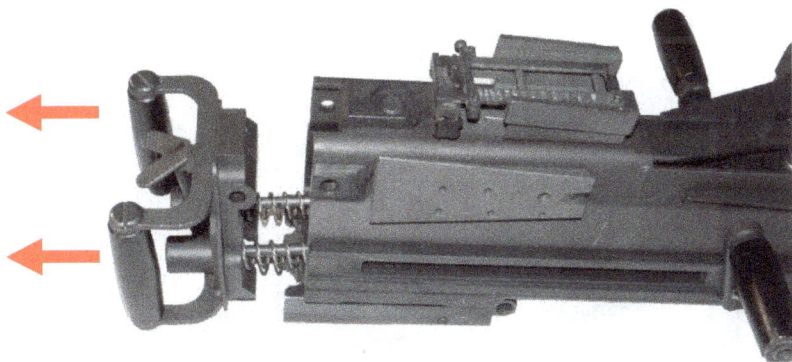

Figure 2-19a Removal of bolt and backplate assembly

Figure 2-19b Bolt and backplate assembly

(9) Take off the primary drive lever and vertical cam.

    (a) Grasp the primary drive lever and vertical cam with one hand and ensure they do not fall when released.

    (b) Reach under the top of the receiver and locate the drive lever lock (Figure 2-20).

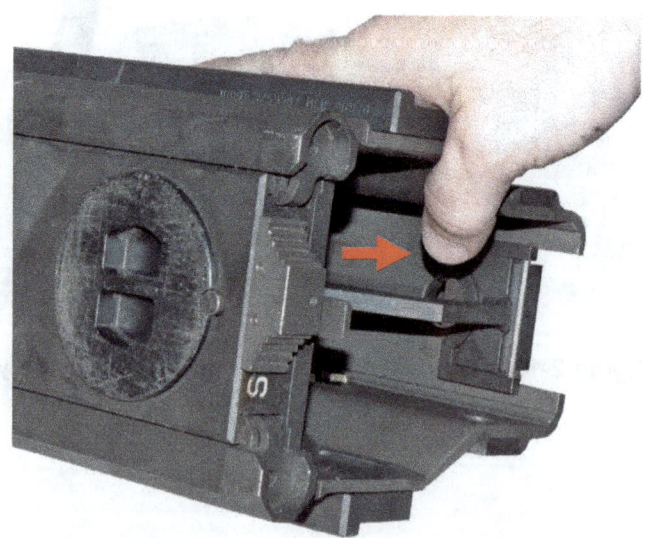

Figure 2-20 Location of drive level lock

    (c) Slide the lock one-quarter of an inch to the rear.

(d) Press down on the primary drive lever pivot post, which releases both the primary drive and vertical cam (Figure 2-21).

Figure 2-21 Primary drive lever removal

(e) Pull the primary drive lever from the front of the weapon and the vertical cam from the back (Figure 2-22).

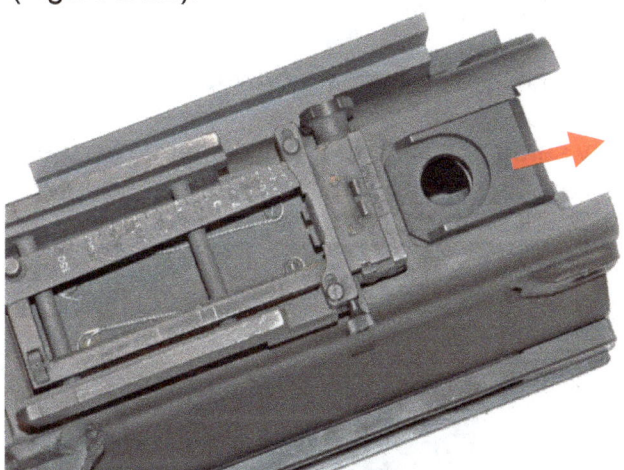

Figure 2-22 Vertical cam removal

CAUTION- Ensure you do not scratch the shiny portion of the vertical cam and primary drive lever. These areas have been specially treated to reduce friction; any scratches or use of abrasives will take off the treatment and increase wear.

(10) Take out the charger assemblies from both sides by following these procedures.

(a) Place the charger assemblies in the upright position.

(b) Using a metal link or spent cartridge case, retract the lock plunger (Figure 2-23a) at the base of the charger arm.

(c) Slide the charger housing rearward to disengage the lugs from the keyslots in the receiver (Figure 2-23b).

(d) Lift the charger assembly away from the receiver.

 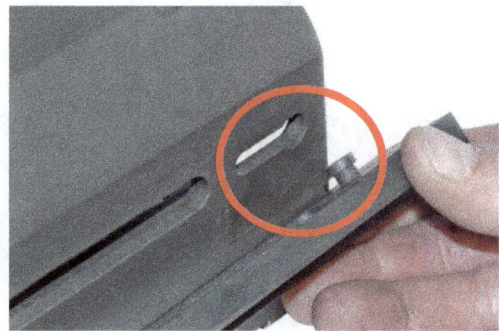

Figure 2-23a   **Figure 2-23b**
Charger assemblies

(11) Take off the sear assembly by following these procedures:

(a) Turn the MK19 on its side or upside down.

(b) Move the safety selector switch to F (FIRE), and use the rim of a spent cartridge case to lift up the sear lock plunger, circled in red (Figure 2-24).

Figure 2-24 Lock plunger location

(c) At the same time, squeeze the sear with your finger and rotate the sear assembly (left or right) until you can no longer hold the sear (Figure 2-25).

Figure 2-25 Rotate the sear assembly

(d) Release the plunger, and apply downward pressure to the sear assembly. (A spring in the sear will push the sear away from the receiver, preventing further turning of the sear.)

(e) With the sear pressed flush to the receiver, continue to turn the sear until you hear a metallic click.

(f) Place the safety selector switch on S (SAFE) and continue to rotate the sear until it is at a 90-degree angle to the receiver (Figure 2-26).

Figure 2-26 Removing the sear assembly

(g) Lift the sear assembly straight off the receiver.

*Practical Guide to the Operational Use of the **MK19 MOD3 Grenade Machine Gun***

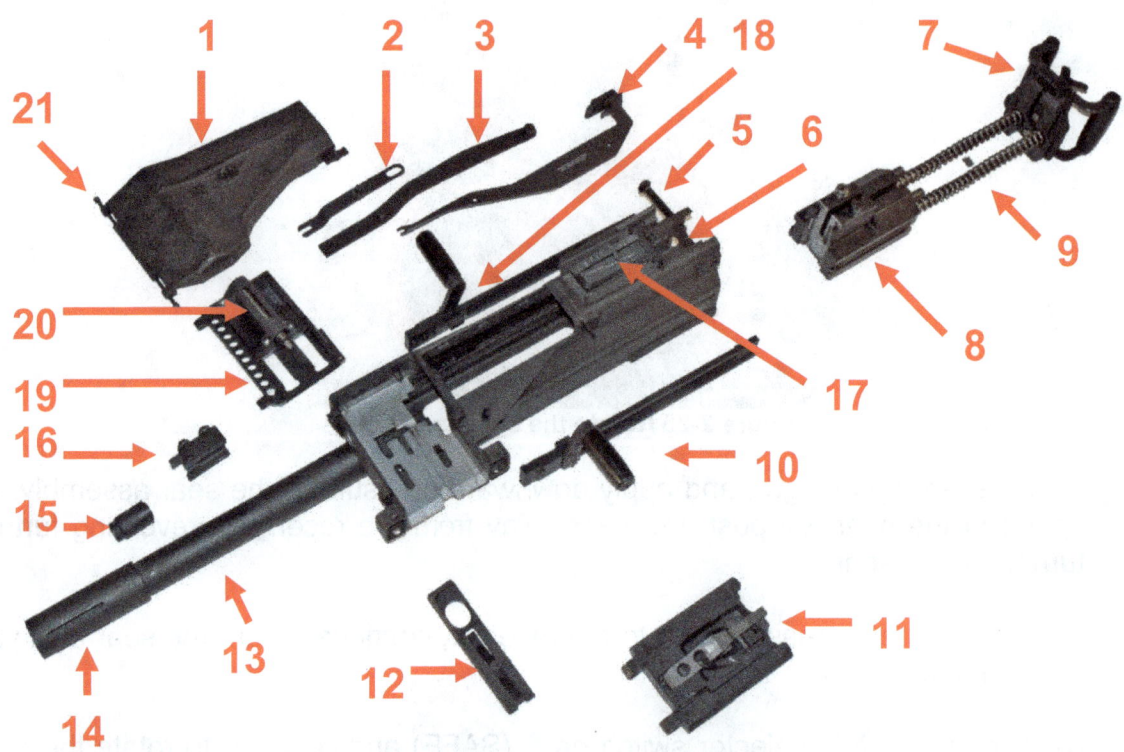

Figure 2-27 Disassembled MK19

1 Top Cover
2 Secondary Drive Lever
3 Primary Drive Lever
4 Vertical Cam Assembly
5 Backplate Pin
6 Receiver Assembly
7 Control Grip Assembly
8 Bolt
9 Guide Rods and Springs
10 Charger Assembly, Left
11 Sear Assemble

12 Alignment Guide Assembly
13 Barrel
14 Flash Suppressor
15 Ogive Plunger Assembly
16 Round-positioning Block
17 Rear Sight Assembly
18 Charger Assembly, Right
19 Feed Tray
20 Feed Slide
21 Cover Pins

Cleaning, Lubrication, and Preventive Maintenance for the MK19

The MK19 requires preventive maintenance checks and services (PMCS) and lubrication before, during, and after firing. It should be checked and cleaned daily when used and not fired, and weekly if not used. For more detailed guidance on the care, cleaning, and PMCS for the MK19, refer to TM 9-1010-230-10.

A. **Cleaning and Lubrication-** Several types of lubricants can be used on the MK19. High-friction areas of the gun have a protective coating, and care must be taken to prevent its removal. Listed below are authorized lubricants and other information about lubricating and cleaning the MK19.

(1) **Authorized Lubricants-** These are the authorized lubricants used on the MK19:

    (a) Lubricant, artic weather, automatic weapons (LAW).

    (b) Lubricating oil, semi fluid, automatic weapons (LSA).

    (c) Lubricating oil, semi fluid, automatic weapons, temperate (LSAT).

    (d) Rifle bore cleaner (RBC). RBC should be used sparingly only in the bore and when necessary.

    (e) Grease, molybdenum disulfide (GMD).

(2) **Use of Lubricants-** The following is general guidance on the use of lubricants on the MK19.

    (a) Never mix lubricants on the MK19. If you change lubricants or do not know for sure which lubricant is currently applied to the MK19, completely clean off all old materials before you apply a new lubricant.

    (b) Never use cleaner lubricant petroleum (CLP) on a MK19. It gums up moving parts instead of lubricating them.

    (c) Apply a heavy coat of lubricant and do not wipe it off.

    (d) In cold weather, 0 degrees F to -25 degrees F, use LSAT, GMD, or LAW.

    (e) In extra cold weather, -25 degrees F and below, use LAW.

(3) **High-friction Areas-** The under side of the primary drive lever, the vertical cam assembly, the bolt (where it rides on the rails), and the area where the feed slide and feed slide tray connect have been treated to prolong the life of the MK19. Special care is required during cleaning and maintenance to prevent damage to the coating. CLP, acids,

and abrasives should never be used on the MK19 because they will remove the protective coating.

B. **General Cleaning and Lubrication Instructions-** The following is general guidance for the cleaning of the MK19.

    (1) Wipe or brush off dirt and grime.

    (2) When lubricating the weapon, give extra attention to the feed pawls, the cocking lever rails, the pivot posts on the primary drive lever, and the bolt assembly.

    (3) Lubricate each part. Give special care to those hard-to-reach spots.

    (4) Work in the lubricant by moving the parts.

C. **When to Clean, Lubricate and Inspect the MK19-** Clean and inspect the gun thoroughly. Report all worn, burred, defective, or missing parts to your armorer or support maintenance. In general, lubricate and clean the MK19 as follows:

(1) Always clean and lubricate the gun after firing.

(2) Clean and lubricate the gun daily if it is used but not fired.

(3) Clean and lubricate the gun weekly if the weapon is stored.

D. **Inspections-** Several parts of the MK19 should be checked whenever possible. These include:

(1) The vertical cam. Check closely for smoothness.

(2) The gap between the charger assemblies and the receiver.

(3) All parts for wear, cracks, missing items, and abnormal shapes.

Figure 2-28a
Sear assembly on SAFE

Figure 2-28b
Sear assembly on FIRE

NOTE disengagement of the safety in relation to the sear.

Assembling the MK19

A. To assemble the gun, replace the groups in the in reverse order of their removal in disassembly. Be sure the components are lubricated prior to reassembly.

(1) Install left and right hand charger assemblies by following these procedures:

    (a) Turn receiver upright.

    (b) Rotate charger handle to the forward straight-up position.

    (c) Line up lugs on charger with slots in receiver rail. Insert charger lugs into slots.

    (d) Hold charger tightly against rail. Slide charger forward until it locks in place.

(2) Install round-positioning block. Insert pins into the slots on the receiver and slide the block forward until the pins lock into the small sections of the holes.

(3) Install the ogive plunger assembly. Insert ogive plunger as shown in Figure 2-16.

(4) Install alignment guide assembly by following these procedures:

    (a) Position the alignment guide assembly so that the pin is lined up with the slot in the feeder wall.

    (b) Hold the alignment guide against the front wall and slide the alignment guide into the receiver until it locks or 'clicks.'

(5) Install feed tray and feed slide assembly by following these procedures (Figure 2-29):

    (a) Place tray into top of feeder, recessed side up. The tabs on the feed slide should align with the slots on the feed slide tray.

    (b) The hinge pinholes on the tray should line up with the hinge pinholes on the receiver.

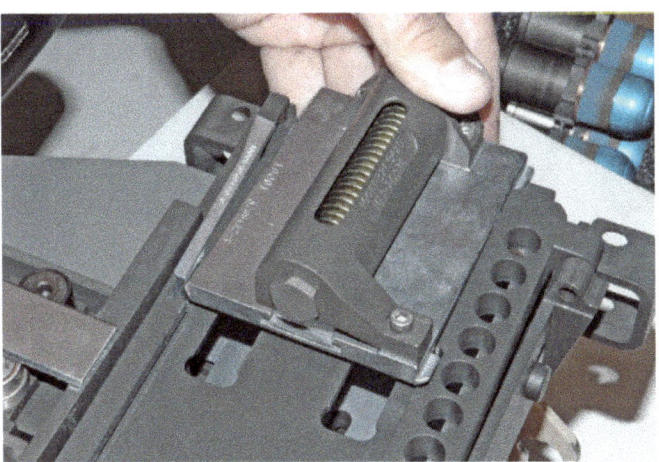

Figure 2-29 Feed slide assembly

(6) Install top cover assembly by following these procedures:

CAUTION- To avoid breaking the cross pin, be sure it is fully inserted into the receiver before closing the top cover.

(a) Feed tray should be in place, resting on the receiver.

(b) Place the top cover on the receiver with the hinge pinholes in line with the receiver lug-end feed-tray hinge pinholes.

(c) Hold top cover at a right angle to the receiver so that the key slots are aligned. Insert top cover pins on both sides. Ensure the cross pin is fully inserted and then rotate the top cover fully open.

(7) Install the secondary drive lever by following these procedures (Figure 2-30):

CAUTION If the secondary drive lever is not properly engaged with the feed slide pin, the gun will not fire.

(a) Rotate the feed slide assembly and tray upward.

(b) Engage the forked end of the secondary drive lever with the feed slide pin.

(c) Press the raised pivot post through the hole in the top cover.

(d) Press the secondary drive lever against the top cover until it locks in place.

Figure 2-30 Installation of the secondary drive lever

(8) Install the vertical cam assembly by following these procedures:

    (a) Slide the vertical cam assembly through the rear of the receiver. The raised portion should slide over the top of the receiver. The drive lever lock should be underneath.

    (b) Engage the forked end in the notch.

(9) Engage the primary drive lever by following these procedures:

    (a) Hold the vertical cam assembly in place and slide the primary drive lever into the receiver and rest the front end on the feed area.

    (b) Slide the drive lever lock rearward and engage the pivot post of lever through holes in the receiver and vertical cam.

    (c) Slide the drive lever lock (on the vertical cam just beneath the top of the receiver) forward.

(10) Install bolt and backplate assembly. With the sear assembly on the gun, assemble the bolt and backplate using the following procedure (Figure 2-31):

CAUTION- Do not damage the vertical cam by hitting it on the inside of the receiver.

CAUTION- Before inserting the assembly, put the cocking lever in forward position.

*Practical Guide to the Operational Use of the **MK19 MOD3 Grenade Machine Gun***

Figure 2-31 Installation of the bolt and backplate assembly

(a) Place safety in F (FIRE) position.

(b) Ensure that the cocking lever is forward, and align the bolt at the rear of the receiver and slide the receiver forward until it stops.

(c) Press down on the bolt release, slide the bolt slightly forward, and remove hands from the bolt release.

(d) Continue to slide the bolt forward until it stops again.

(e) Again, press down on the bolt release, slide the bolt slightly forward, and remove hands from the bolt release.

(f) Continue to slide the bolt forward until it reaches its most forward position.

(g) Seat the bottom of the backplate into the slots on the bottom of the receiver.

(h) Insert the backplate pin to lock the assembly in place.

(11) Install the sear assembly by following these procedures:

(a) Turn the receiver over on its top.

(b) Place the sear housing on the receiver and line up sear housing assembly at a right angle to the barrel centerline.

(c) Put safety on F (FIRE) position.

(d) Press down and rotate the sear assembly until it locks in place.

(12) Install feed throat assembly by following these procedures:

(a) Squeeze the plungers, and align the pins with the holes in the receiver.

(b) Release plunger to reattach feed throat.

NOTE- Ensure the safety switch is in the F (FIRE) position so the sear can be easily depressed.

Function Check Procedures

WARNING
Before performing any procedure, make sure the weapon is clear of ammunition.

A. Check the functioning of the safety switch.
   1) With the cover closed, place safety switch on safe (S).
   2) Pull the bolt to rear, push charger handles to forward position, and rotate handles up.
   3) Press the trigger. The bolt should not go forward.
   4) Place the safety switch on F (FIRE) position.
   5) Press the trigger. The bolt should spring forward.
   6) Place the safety switch on S (SAFE) and leave the bolt in the forward position.

B. Open top cover assembly and inspect the feed tray assembly and the chamber to ensure the gun is clear.
   1) Open the top cover.
   2) Touch the firing pin. If it is not protruding, recharge and release the bolt spring under pressure.
   3) Inspect the bolt face to make sure it is not worn, dirty, pitted, corroded, or in need of lubrication.

WARNING
Do not allow the top cover to slam shut from the raised position. Doing so could injure your hand or damage the equipment.

C. Check the feed slide assembly and feeder.
   1) Move the secondary drive lever back and forth. The feed slide assembly should move freely.
   2) Press the feed pawls to check for spring pressure.
   3) Inspect the link guide for roughness and galling.

Note- Before closing the top cover, always make sure that the secondary drive lever is engaged with the feed slide pin. The feed slide assembly is to the left. The bolt is forward.

Note- Never try to force the top cover closed. Doing so could damage the equipment.
   4) Close and latch the top cover.

D. If you find any deficiencies that you cannot correct, the MK19 is unserviceable. Report the deficiencies to your supervisor.

Section 3

Operation and Function

Safety

The paramount consideration while training with the machine gun is safety. It is imperative that the weapon be cleared properly before disassembly and inspection.

Weapons Conditions

A. <u>Condition 1</u>: Ammunition is in the position on the feed tray with the cover closed. The weapon has been charged twice. The bolt is locked to the rear, and the safety is on **SAFE**.

B. <u>Condition 2</u>: This weapon condition does not apply to the MK19.

C. <u>Condition 3</u>: Ammunition is in the position on the feed tray with the cover closed. The weapon has been charged once. The chamber is empty. The bolt is forward, and the safety is on **SAFE**.

D. <u>Condition 4</u>: The feed tray is clear of ammunition, the chamber is empty, the bolt is forward, and the safety is on **SAFE**.

Clearing the MK19 in Condition 1

The MK19 is cleared differently in a firing situation than in a non-firing situation.

Firing Situation. In a firing situation, use the following procedures to clear the MK19:

(1) Move the safety switch to S (SAFE) (Figure 3-1).

Figure 3-1 S (SAFE) position

(2) Open the top cover assembly (Figure 3-2) by rotating the feed tray cover latch and lifting the feed tray forward. If all the ammunition has NOT been fired, the bolt is to the rear, and a round is on the bolt face. If the bolt is forward, lock it to the rear.

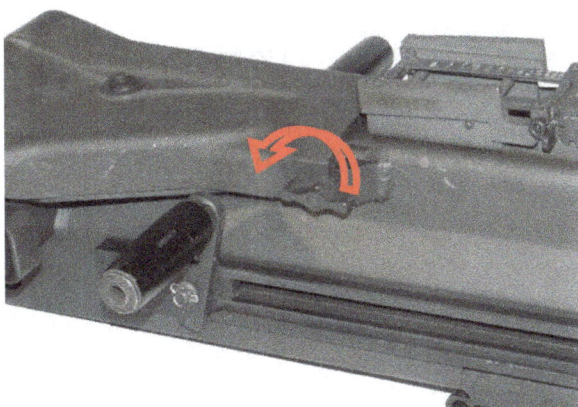

Figure 3-2 Opening the top cover assembly

(3) Take the ammunition from the feed tray by reaching beneath the feed tray and pressing the primary and secondary positioning pawls. While pressing the position pawls, slide the linked rounds out of the MK19 through the feed throat (Figure 3-3a).

Figure 3-3a Removal of linked rounds from feeder

(4) Insert a section of the cleaning rod or bayonet through either side of the receiver rail. Place it on top of the live round or cartridge case, as close to the bolt face as possible, and push down (Figure 3-3b). This action forces the round out of the MK19.

Figure 3-3b Use of a cleaning rod to remove round from bolt face

(5) Lower (1) the charging handles on both sides by pressing in the lock to rotate (2) the handles down and then pull (3) both charger handles to the rear
 (Figure 3-4).

Figure 3-4 Charger handles

(6) Inspect the chamber and bolt face to ensure that no live rounds are in the weapon.

(7) Place the safety switch on F (FIRE) (Figure 3-5).

Figure 3-5 Safety in FIRE position

(8) <u>Maintain rearward pressure on the charging handle</u>, press the trigger, and ease the bolt forward (Figure 3-6).

Figure 3-6 Pressing the trigger to release the bolt

(9) Place the safety switch on S (SAFE) (Figure 3-7).

Figure 3-7 S (SAFE) position

Clearing the MK19 in Condition 4

Non-firing Situation. In a non-firing situation, use the following procedures to clear the MK19:
    (1) Place the safety switch on S (SAFE).
    (2) Open the top cover assembly.
    (3) Lower one or both charger handles.
    (4) Pull the charger handle slightly to the rear.
    (5) Allow sufficient space between the face of the bolt and the chamber to see both.
    (6) Check for live ammunition.
    (7) Ride the bolt forward.
    (8) Return the charger handle to its original upright position.

Cycle of Operation

The MK19's cycle of operation includes six steps: charging, extracting (delinking), cocking, firing, blowback, and automatic feeding. More than one step may be done at the same time.

A. **Charging-** The charger handles are used to pull the bolt (1) to the rear, aligning the round with the bolt extractors. The rearward movement of the bolt causes the primary drive lever (2) to move to the left, which moves the secondary drive lever (3) to the right. The forked end of the secondary drive lever, which rests on the feed slide pin (4), moves the feed slide (5) to the right. The feed pawls (6) on the feed slide move the linked rounds (7) over one place in the ammunition-feed area of the receiver. The leading round (8) lines up with the bolt extractor (9). See Figure 3-8.

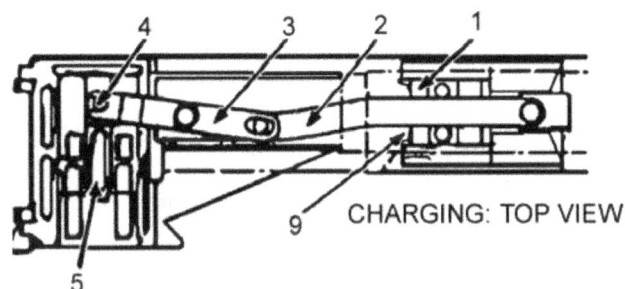

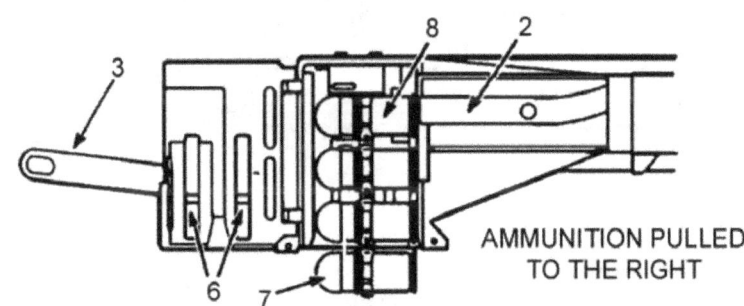

Figure 3-8 Charging cycle

B. **Extracting (Delinking)-** When a round is stripped from the belt, it is extracted or "delinked." This happens, after the MK19 has been charged once, when the trigger (10) is pressed. The bolt slams forward and the bolt's extractors (11) snap over the rim of the cartridge case. When the MK19 is charged again, the extractor pulls the leading round to the rear and separates the male and female links. The curved edge of the vertical cam (12) forces the lead round out of the extractors and into the bolt fingers (13). With the bolt completely to the rear, the round lines up with the chamber (14), and is ready to fire. As the original leading round chambers, the next round aligns with the bolt extractors. See Figure 3-9.

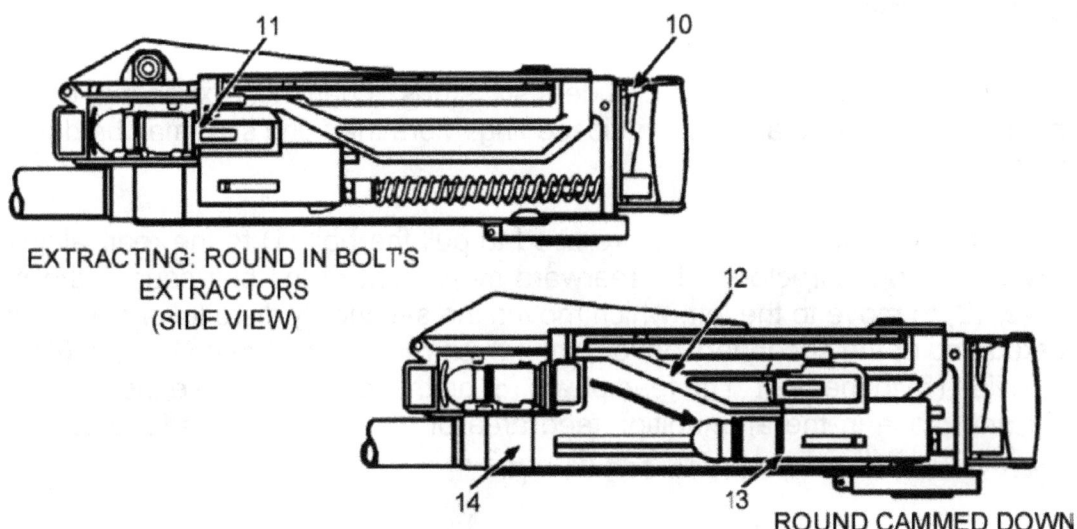

Figure 3-9 Extracting (delinking) round

C. **Cocking-** The rearward movement of the bolt causes the cocking lever (15) to retract the firing pin (16). When the cocking lever hits the rear end of the left receiver rail slot (17), the cocking lever is forced forward. When the cocking lever retracts the firing pin, the firing pin sear holds the firing pin to the rear (18). See Figure 3-10.

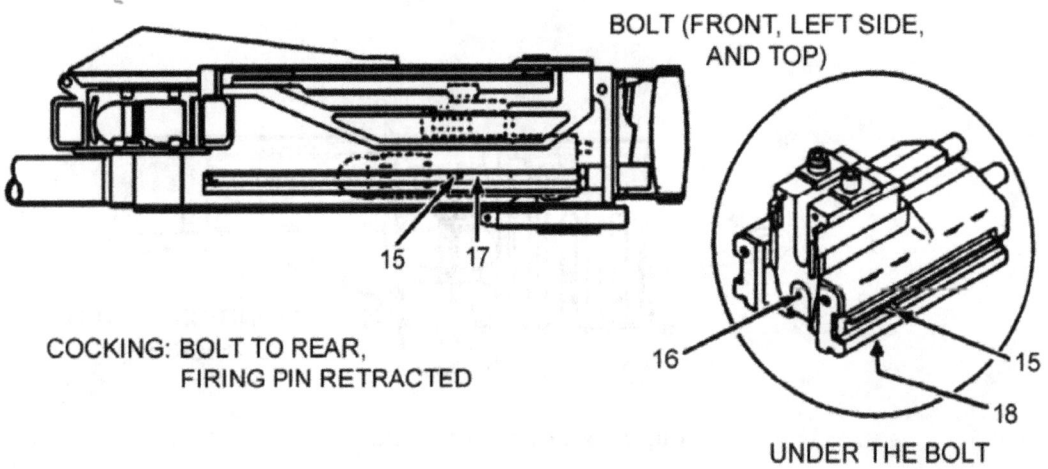

Figure 3-10 Cocking the MK19

D. **Firing Cycle-** The safety switch is on F (FIRE). Pressing the trigger (20) depresses the tip of the receiver sear (21). The receiver sear disengages the bolt sear (22), which releases the bolt forward under spring pressure with a round in the bolt fingers. The cocking lever hits the forward end of the left receiver rail slot, forcing the lever to the rear. The bolt sear hits a plate in the bottom of the receiver, which pushes the firing pin sear up to release the firing pin. A combination of the bolt's inertia and pressure from the firing pin spring drive the firing pin forward. The tip of the firing pin detonates the primer. The round is not completely inside the chamber at the moment the weapon is fired. The cartridge case, held by the bolt fingers, protrudes from the chamber (23). The explosion forces the projectile down the bore. See Figure 3-11.

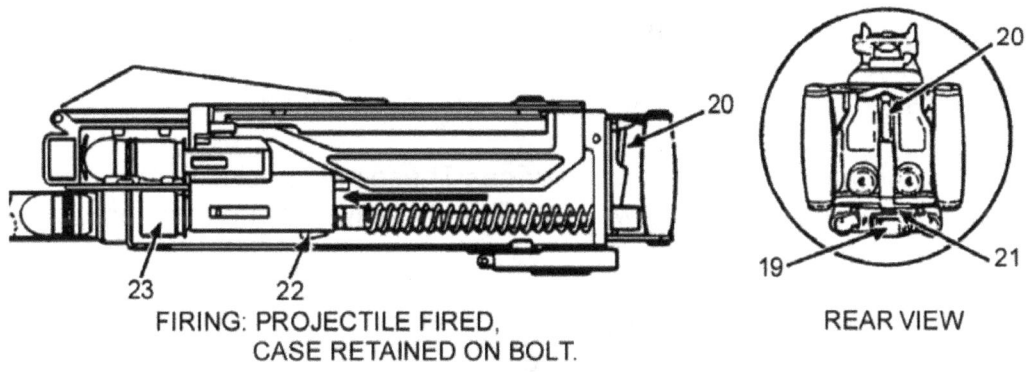

FIRING: PROJECTILE FIRED,
CASE RETAINED ON BOLT.

REAR VIEW

Figure 3-11 Firing cycle

E. **Blowback and Automatic Feeding Cycle-** The gases from the burning powder force the bolt, with a new round in its extractors, to the rear. During this blowback, several things happen at once. First, the curved rail of the vertical cam delinks and forces down the new round on top of the spent case, which forces the spent case out of the bolt fingers and ejects it out the bottom of the gun. Next, the feed slide assembly pulls the rounds to the right in the receiver ammunition feed area, where a new round is ready to pick up (automatic feed). During the bolt's travel to the rear, the cocking lever is pushed forward, which cocks the firing pin. When the bolt reaches the limit of its rearward travel, the recoil springs (24) are completely compressed. The bolt buffers (25) absorb over-travel, reducing trunnion load (recoil force) at the gun-mount attaching points. The bolt sear will not engage the receiver sear if the trigger is still depressed, and another firing cycle occurs. Release of the trigger causes the bolt sear to engage the receiver sear, which prevents the bolt from going forward, and firing stops. See Figure 3-12.

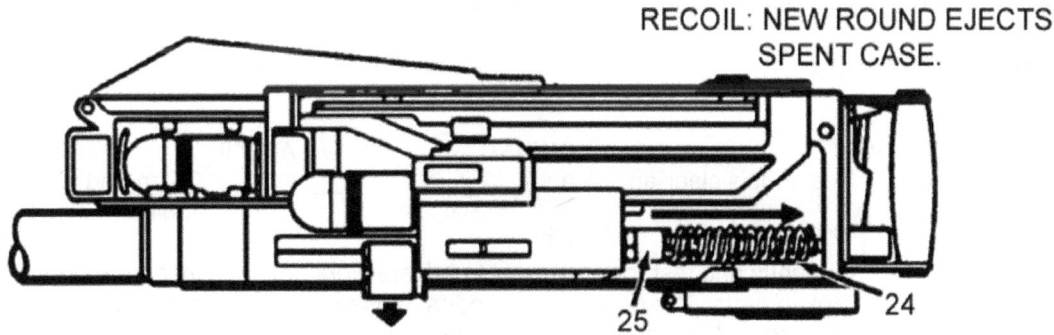

RECOIL: NEW ROUND EJECTS SPENT CASE.

Figure 3-12 Blowback and automatic feed

Practical Guide to the Operational Use of the **MK19 MOD3 Grenade Machine Gun**

Operation

The overall section on the operation of the MK19 includes how to load, unload, and clear the weapon. During the weapon's operation, it is mandatory that all ammunition be free of dirt and corrosion, and that the ammunition be properly linked.

Operational maintenance checks and services These are checks that the gunner must perform before he can safely fire the weapon. They are divided into three groups: before, during, and after firing checks.

A. Before firing the weapon, ensure that:
    (1) The correct ammunition is on hand.
    (2) The ammunition is clean and dent-free.
    (3) All ogives on the cartridges are tight.
    (4) The line of fire is clear of obstructions.

B. While firing the weapon, ensure that:
    (1) The top cover is closed.
    (2) The muzzle of the MK19 is pointed downrange at all times.

NOTE- In the event of a runaway gun, lower one of the charging handles.

    (3) Use the suggested three to five-round bursts.

C. After firing the weapon:
    (1) Unload and clear the MK19.
    (2) Note weapon discrepancies and report them to the armorer.
    (3) Clean and lubricate the MK19 before storage.

Operations Checklist

WEAPON PART	BEFORE	DURING	AFTER
1. Bore	Ensure it is clear and clean.	_____	Clean and oil lightly.
2. Moving parts	Oil lightly and test for worn or broken parts. The moving parts should function without excessive friction.	Lubricate working parts. Observe the functioning of the gun to anticipate failures.	Inspect, clean, and oil lightly.
3. Ammunition	a. Ensure the correct type of ammunition is used. b. Ensure the ammunition is clean and dent free. c. Ensure all ogives are tight. d. Have an adequate supply of	Keep correctly aligned in the feedtray. Check resupply. Protect from sun, moisture, and dirt. Watch for link stoppage.	Clean, store carefully, and replenish supply.

		ammunition on hand.	
4. Top cover	Inspect the top cover for dents or damage.	Keep closed and locked down.	Lube properly after cleaning.
5. Line of fire	Ensure the line of fire is clear of all obstructions.	Cease fire if any obstruction appears in the line of fire.	_____

Ground and Vehicle Mounts

The MK19 can be mounted on the ground or on a vehicle. The M3 tripod, the most often used ground mount, allows the gunner to fire the weapon in a stable manner from any angle. The MK64, MOD 7 gun cradle allows the MK19 to be mounted on any vehicle equipped for the M2 caliber .50 machine gun; these vehicles include the 2 1/2 and 5-ton cargo trucks, high-mobility multi-purpose wheeled vehicle (HMMWV), M113-series armored personnel carrier (APC), and other more modernized currently used vehicles. This chapter discusses both the ground- and vehicle-mounting procedures.

MK64 Mod 7 Gun Cradle

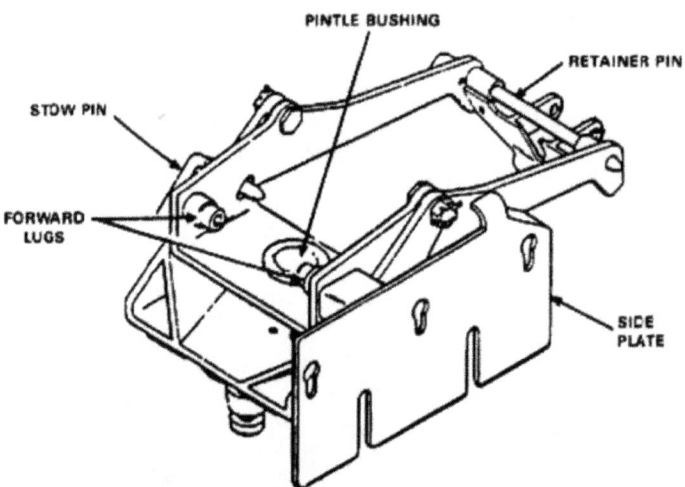

Figure 3-13 MK64 Mod 7 Gun Cradle

Use the MK64 gun cradle to mount the MK19 to the gun pedestal, stand, ring, or tripod. Attach the ammunition container bracket to the side plate of the cradle. In the center of the cradle is a pintle bushing and lock in which the M2 caliber .50 and M60 guns can be mounted. The front of the MK19 is mounted on the two forward lugs of the gun cradle; the retainer pin secures the MK19's rear. Insert the cradle stow pin to hold the cradle in a horizontal position during travel (Figure 3-13).

MK 93 Gun Cradle

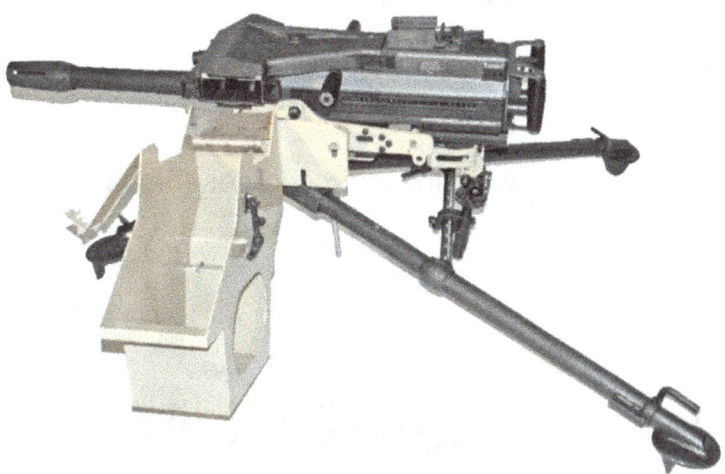

Figure 3-14 MK93

This MK93 Machine Gun Mount is a new (2004) stronger design by the U.S. Army. The mount accepts the M2HB 12.7mm machine gun or the MK19 40mm machine gun and is designed for use on HMMWVs, trucks and armored vehicles. With its small pintle, it fits into a variety of tripods, pedestals, and the Universal Pintle Adapter (UPA). The left rail supports an interface plate that accepts a variety of quick-removable ammo can holders. The M2HB weapon is held in place by front and rear stainless-steel ball lock pins. A slider system with two hydraulic shock absorbers reduces firing shock in both recoil and counter recoil for the M2HB. The normal recoil of 1200 pounds is reduced to under 500 pounds peak.

The MK19 weapon that has internal shock absorbers is held in place with a stainless-steel rear pin and two studs in front, allowing the weapon to slide back and forth in the mount. A train stop block and depression stop assembly provide travel stop limits. An elevation travel lock pin locks the carriage to the cradle, making it much easier to install a weapon. Holes in the carriage are provided for installation of armor brackets and Armor Shield (M35-021).

An optional Adapter Kit (M35-800) manufactured by Military Systems Group, provides for installation of the M240 or the M249 weapons. It is not recommended to use this Machine Gun Mount with the Swing Arm system or in Naval applications due to its fabrication using carbon steel.

Ground-mount using the M3 Tripod

Mount the MK19 as close to the ground as possible and lock the tripod's trail legs open. Set the adjustable front tripod leg to an angle of about 60 degrees to the ground. For example, in flat terrain with the extensions closed, use the following method to place the MK19 about 12 inches above the ground.

A. Set the tripod trail legs by following these procedures (Figure 3-15):

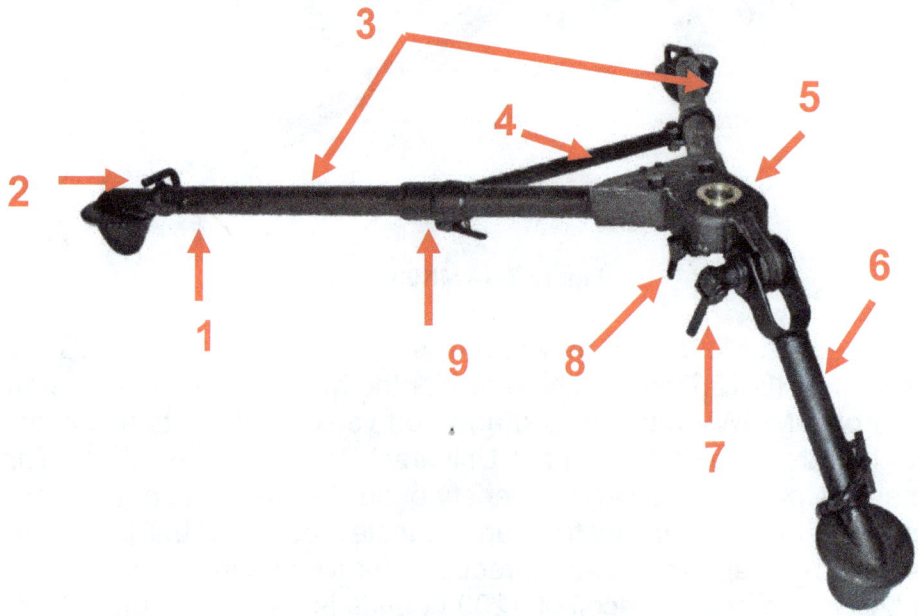

Figure 3-15 M3 Tripod

1 – Indexing Lever Assembly
2 – Leg Clamping Handle
3 – Trail Legs
4 – Traversing Bar
5 – Tripod Head
6 – Front Leg
7 – Front Leg Clamp Handle
8 – Pintle Lock Release Cam
9 – Rear Right Leg Sliding Sleeve

(1) Unscrew the leg-clamping handle; press down on the indexing lever, and extend the leg to the desired length.

(2) Align the indexing lever stud with one of the holes in the tripod leg extension.

(3) Release pressure on the indexing lever, allowing the stud to fit the desired hole. Tighten the leg-clamping handle.

B. Set the front leg of the tripod by following these procedures:

(1) Turn the front leg clamp handle counterclockwise to loosen the front leg.

(2) Adjust the leg to the desired angle, ensuring the tripod head is level, and tighten the front leg clamp.

C. Secure the tripod legs by following these procedures:

(1) Stamp the metal shoe on each tripod leg into the ground.

(2) Sandbag each leg to stabilize the MK19 for firing.

D. Mount the M64 gun cradle onto the M3 tripod by following these procedures:

(1) Unlock the tripod pintle lock release cam.

(2) Insert the gun cradle's pintle into the tripod pintle bushing (Figure 3-16).

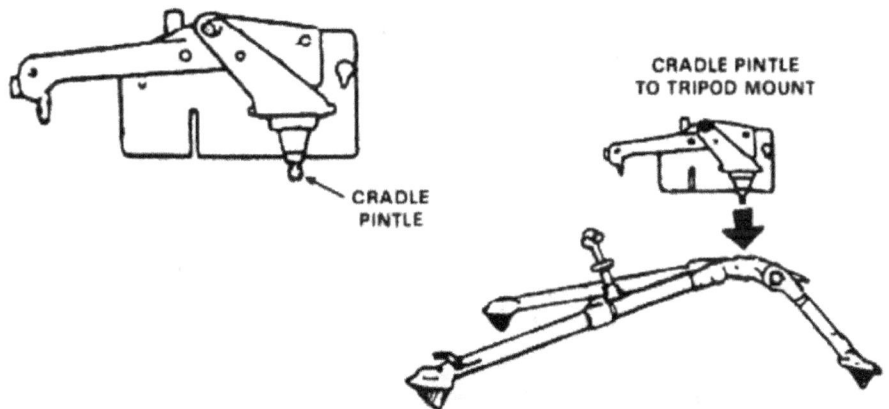

Figure 3-16 Insertion of pintle into pintle bushing

(3) Lock the pintle lock release cam to secure the gun cradle. Check the gun cradle, by pulling up on it slightly, to ensure that it is seated and locked.

E. Attach the T&E (traverse and elevating) mechanism by following these procedures (Figure 3-17):

(1) Zero the T&E mechanism by zeroing the traversing handwheel, elevating handwheel, and the elevating mechanism sleeve to the lower elevating screw.

   (a) To zero the traversing handwheel, hold the T&E mechanism so that the traversing handwheel is on the left when looking at it, and then turn the traversing handwheel toward you until it stops. Loosen the locking nut slightly. Align the zero on the scale with the zero on the elevating screw yoke. Hold the scale with the zeros aligned, and tighten the locking nut. Make sure the zeros stay aligned. Turn the traversing handwheel two complete revolutions away from you. If doing this at night, count 50 "clicks" away from you.

(b) To zero the elevating handwheel to the upper elevating screw, align the two zeros. Rotate the elevating handwheel up or down until a zero with a line below it is visible on the upper elevating screw. Position the elevating handwheel so the indicator is pointing at the zero on the handwheel.

(c) Zero the elevating mechanism sleeve to the lower elevating screw. Rotate the elevating mechanism sleeve all the way up; rotate it down until it stops and note the number of complete turns. Rotate the elevating mechanism sleeve up half that number of turns. Position the slide lock lever to face you.

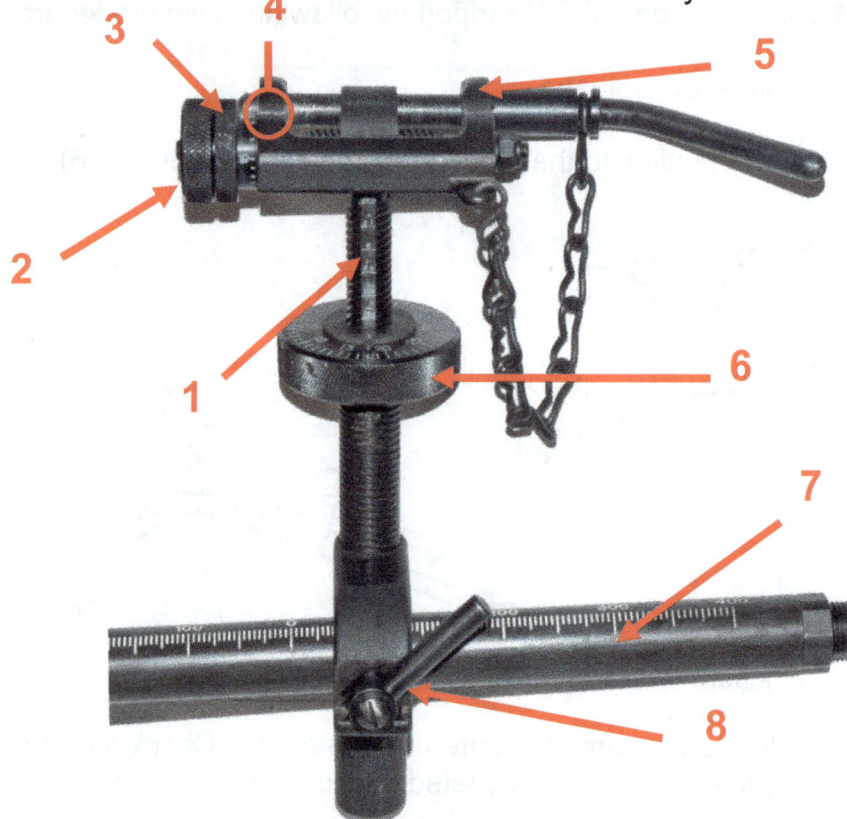

Figure 3-17 T&E Mechanism

1 – Elevation Screw Scale Plate
2 – Traversing Handwheel
3 – Locking Nut
4 – Scale
5 – Yoke
6 – Elevation Handwheel
7 – Traversing Bar
8 – Traversing Bar Lock

(2) Remove the stow pin from the gun cradle (Figure 3-18).

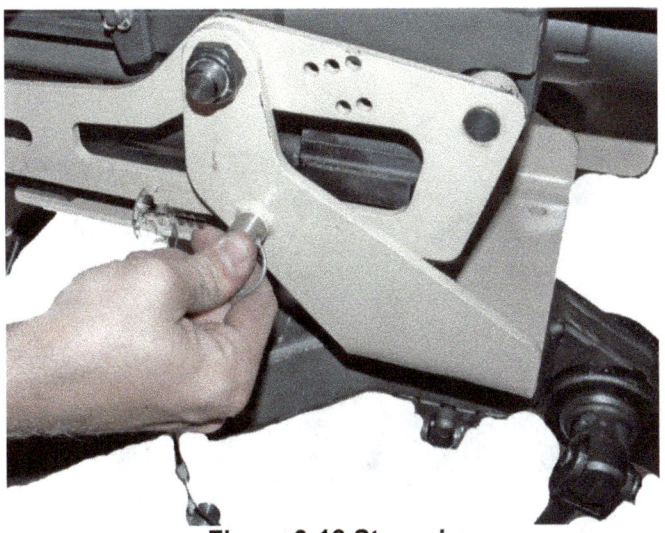
Figure 3-18 Stow pin

(3) Align holes in the upper elevating screw yoke of the T&E mechanism with the rear holes in the gun cradle (Figure 3-19).

NOTE- The stow pin locks the cradle in a horizontal position, preventing it from depressing or elevating.

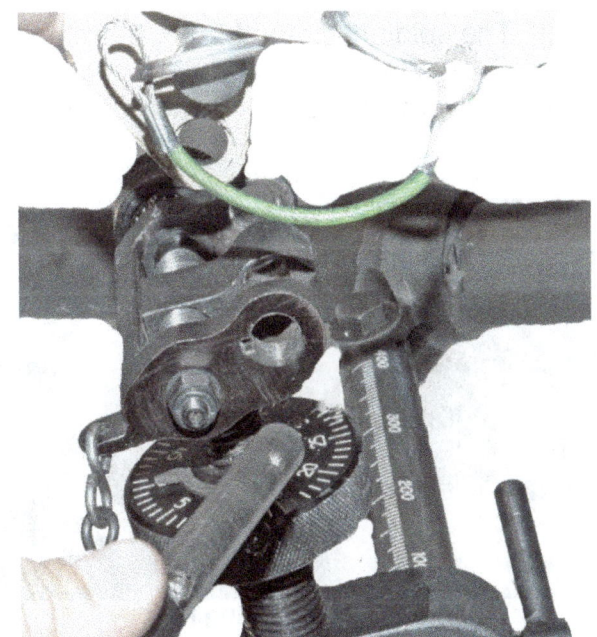
Figure 3-19 Alignment of gun cradle to T&E mechanism

(4) Lock the elevating sleeve mechanism onto the center of the traversing bar.

(5) Insert the quick-release pin from the right (Figure 3-20).

Figure 3-20 Quick-release pin

F. Mount the MK19 by following these procedures:

(1) Lift the MK19 into the gun cradle. One soldier holds the barrel while another holds the control grips. The one holding the grips stands between the trail legs of the tripod; the other straddles the front leg. The soldiers lift the MK19, barrel first, onto the cradle.

(2) Align the grooves on the receiver with the lugs in the gun cradle, and slide the receiver forward (Figure 3-21).

Figure 3-21 Mounting lugs

(3) Align the sear mounting holes with the gun cradle mounting holes (Figure 3-22). Secure the rear of the receiver by inserting the retaining pin through the cradle and sear assembly and rotate it until it locks in place (Figure 3-23). If a safety clip is attached, use it to secure the retaining pin.

Figure 3-22 Alignment of the sear assembly and pinholes

Figure 3-23 Insertion of the cradle retaining pin

G. Attach the feed throat to the MK19 by following these procedures:

(1) Squeeze together each set of grip pins (Figure 3-24).

(2) Attach the feed throat to the front left-hand side of the receiver assembly. The pins of the feed throat must line up with the pinholes in the receiver (Figure 3-25).

(3) Relax pressure on the spring-loaded grip pins so they will snap into place (Figure 3-26).

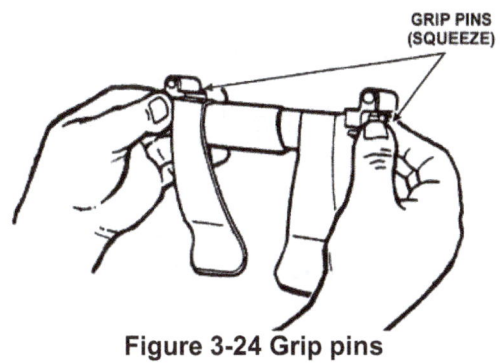

Figure 3-24 Grip pins

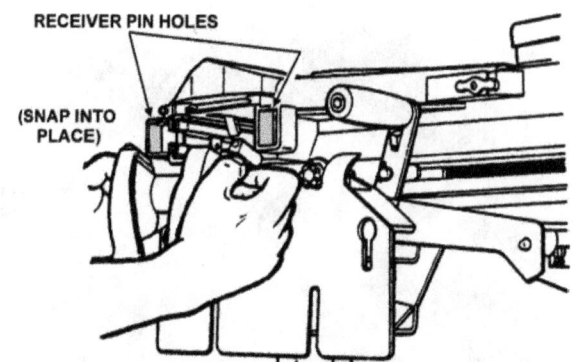
Figure 3-25 Feed throat alignment

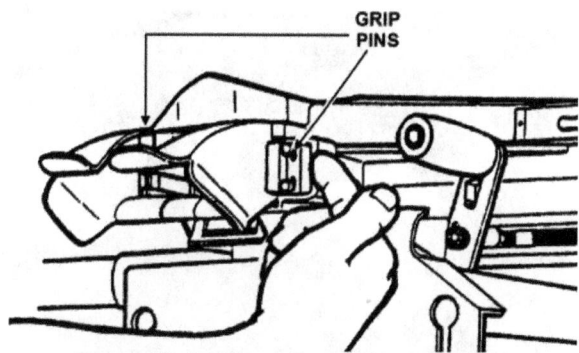
Figure 3-26 Feed throat installation

NOTE- 1. When the MK19 is mounted on the M3 tripod or any vehicle, it is called a weapon system.

2. The same procedure is used to mount the MK19 to the gun cradle regardless of the type of mount used.

Vehicle-mount

This section lists the accessories used and outlines the steps to mount the MK19 onto vehicles. Since mounting procedures for vehicles vary little, this section explains in detail how to mount the MK19 on the HMMWV and highlights the differences in mounting procedures for other vehicles.

A. **Accessories.** Mounting the MK19 on vehicles requires several accessories.

(1) **Gun Cradle.** The MK64 gun cradle is used to mount the MK19 onto any vehicle having a pedestal mount for the M2 machine gun.

(2) **Pintle Adapter.** The pintle adapter is used to mount the MK19 in all vehicular modes (Figure 3-27). Other accessories are used to mount the MK19 to specific vehicles. The upper end accepts the gun cradle's pintle, which is secured by a quick-release pin. The

lower end of the adapter fits the mounting wells on the M4 pedestal, HMMWV weapon platform, M36A2 ring mount with M66 ring, and commander's cupola on the M113 APC.

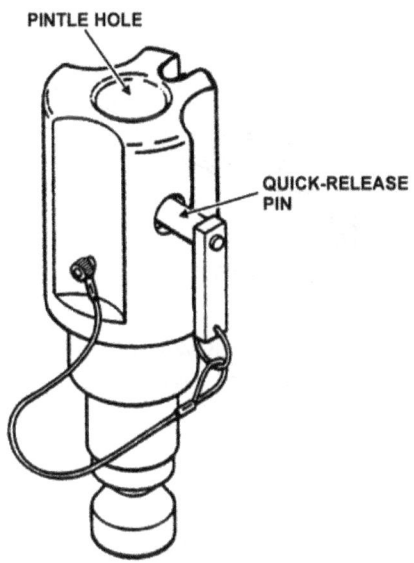

Figure 3-27 Pintle adapter

(3) **Train and Elevating Assembly.** This assembly secures the MK64 gun cradle to the M4 pedestal or HMMWV weapon platform pedestal and allows directional adjustments. The lower end of the train and elevating assembly is attached to the pedestal by a train lock clamp. The clamp is released or locked in position by a train lock handle. Two positioning clamps are supplied to prevent vertical movement of the train lock clamp on the M4 pedestal. When used on the HMMWV weapon platform pedestal, only one clamp is needed above the train lock clamp. The upper end of the train and elevating assembly is a standard caliber .50 T&E mechanism, and it is attached to the lower rear holes in the M4 cradle by a retaining pin (Figure 3-28).

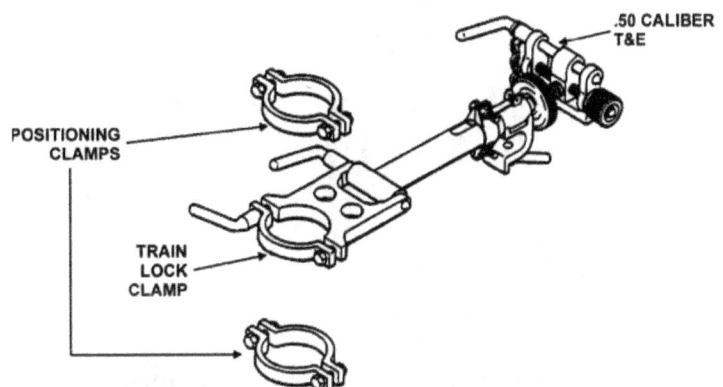

Figure 3-28 Train and elevating assembly

(4) **Travel Lock Adapter.** This adapter is used to hold the gun cradle securely during travel. It is attached to the gun cradle by a retaining pin, which is inserted through the gun cradle train and elevating mechanism mounting holes (Figure 3-29).

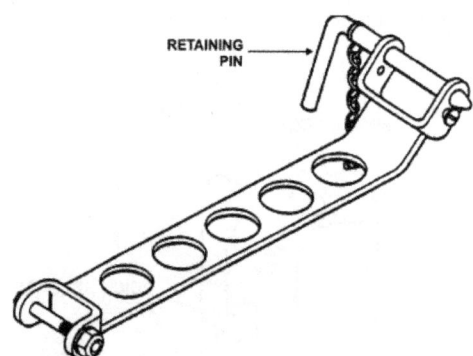

Figure 3-29 Travel lock adapter

(5) **Travel Lock Bracket.** This bracket allows the travel lock adapter to be used with the M4 pedestal mount. It has two halves that are secured around the pedestal with nuts and bolts. The bracket is attached to the travel lock adapter by aligning the lower holes (Figure 3-30).

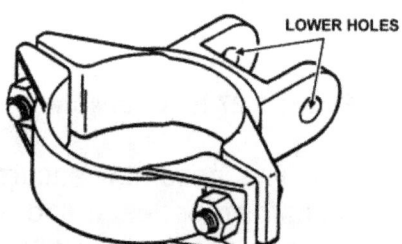

Figure 3-30 Travel lock bracket

(6) **Bracket Mounting Assembly.** This assembly supplies a mount for the M548 metal ammunition container. It has a metal frame that attaches to the gun cradle, and a retaining pin that inserts through the top-inner end of the M548 ammunition container (Figure 3-31).

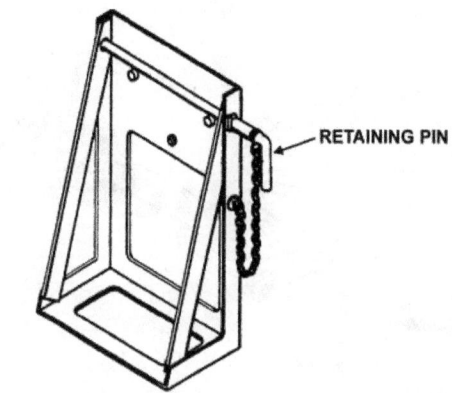

Figure 3-31 Bracket mounting assembly

(7) **Empty Case Catch Bag.** This rubberized canvas bag catches empty cartridge cases as they are ejected. It is held in place by a metal rim, which attaches to the bottom of the cradle under the receiver by two hooks and a hanger (Figure 3-32).

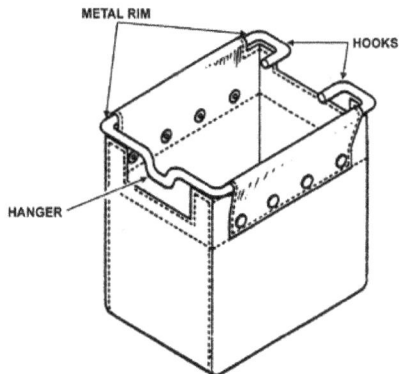

Figure 3-32 Empty case catch bag

NOTE- The 9/16-, 7/16-, and 3/8-inch open-end wrenches are necessary tools to mount the MK19 on vehicles.

B. **Vehicle Mounts.** Various vehicle mounts can be used with the MK19.

(1) **HMMWV Weapon Platform.** To mount the MK19 on the HMMWV weapon platform (Figure 3-33):

(a) Insert the pintle adapter onto the HMMWV pedestal by following these procedures:

(1) Loosen the HMMWV pedestal lock screws by turning counterclockwise until the threaded ends are flushed with the pedestal's inner wall (Figure 3-33).

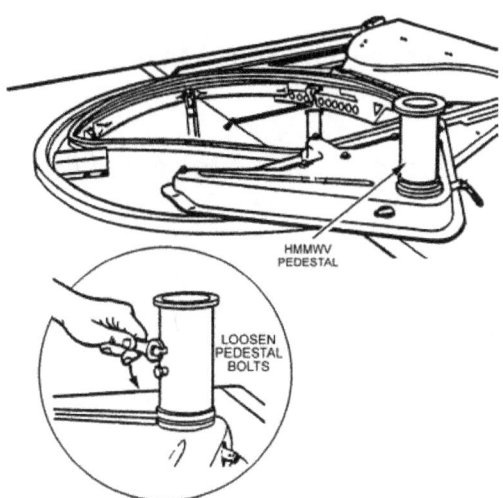

Figure 3-33 HMMWV pedestal

(2) Insert the pintle adapter assembly by placing the lower end of the pintle adapter into the HMMWV pedestal (Figure 3-34).

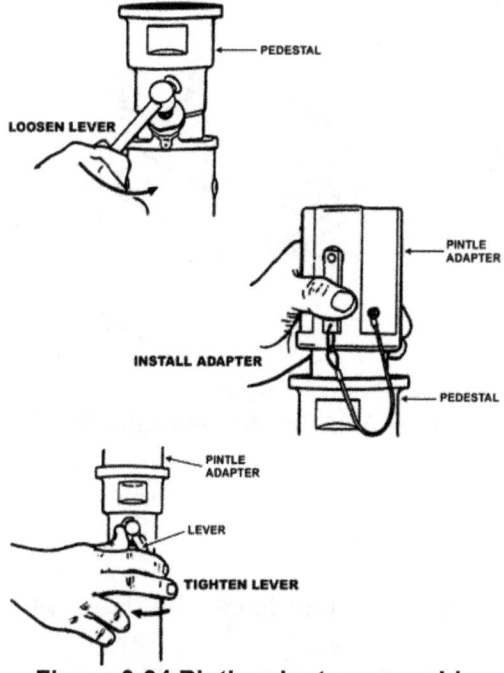

Figure 3-34 Pintle adapter assembly

(3) Tighten the lock screws with a 3/8-inch open-end wrench. Pull upward on the pintle adapter to ensure it is secured in place.

(4) Remove the pintle adapter quick-release by pressing in on the pin's quick-release button and pulling the pin from the pintle adapter.

(b) Install the carriage and cradle assembly by following these procedures (Figure 3-35):

(1) Insert the front stow pin to prevent relative movement to the carriage and cradle.

(2) Insert the carriage pintle into the top of the pintle adapter assembly.

(3) Press in on the pin's quick-release button and insert the pin.

(4) Pull upward and twist the carriage and cradle assembly. It should lock into the pintle adapter, but it should traverse freely left and right.

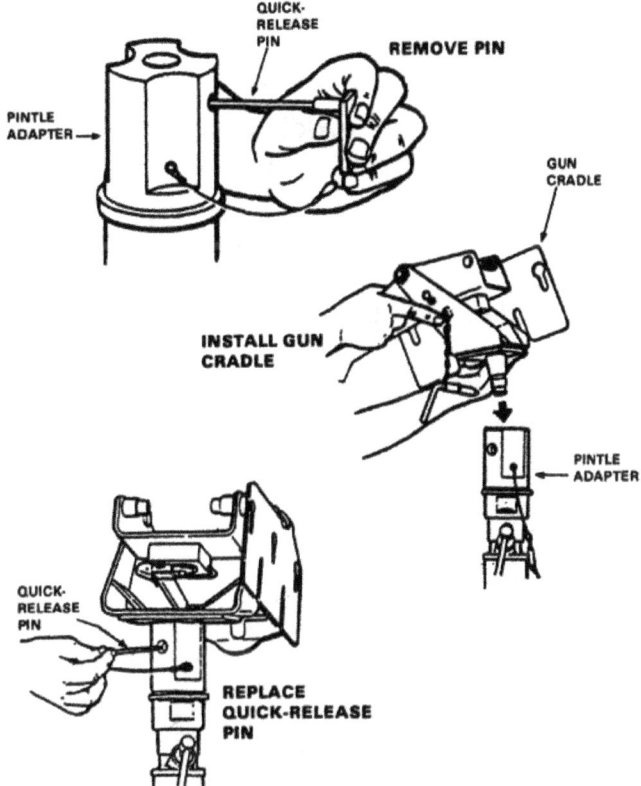

Figure 3-35 Installing the carriage and cradle assembly

(c) Install the T&E mechanism in the train and elevation assembly by following these procedures:

(1) Turn the elevating handwheel to read 250 mils.

(2) Loosen the pivot arm screws, using two 7/16-inch open-end wrenches.

(3) Insert the T&E mechanism all the way into the train and elevation assembly.

NOTE- The T&E mechanism is the upper portion of the training and elevation assembly; it must be installed in the train and elevation assembly before the training and elevation assembly can be installed on the vehicle.

(4) Position the traversing lock lever to the rear and the traversing knob to the left by tightening the pivot arm screws, using the two wrenches.

(d) Separate the middle clamp on the train and elevation assembly by following these procedures:

(1) Unscrew the train lock handle counterclockwise to remove.

(2) Using the 9/16-inch open-end wrench, remove the hex head screw on the other side of the middle clamp.

(e) Attach the train and elevation middle clamp to the HMMWV pedestal post by following these procedures (Figure 3-36):

(1) Assemble the middle clamp around the pedestal.

(2) Tighten the clamp by turning the train lock handle clockwise.

(3) Using the 9/16-inch open-end wrench, equally tighten the screw on the other side of the middle clamp.

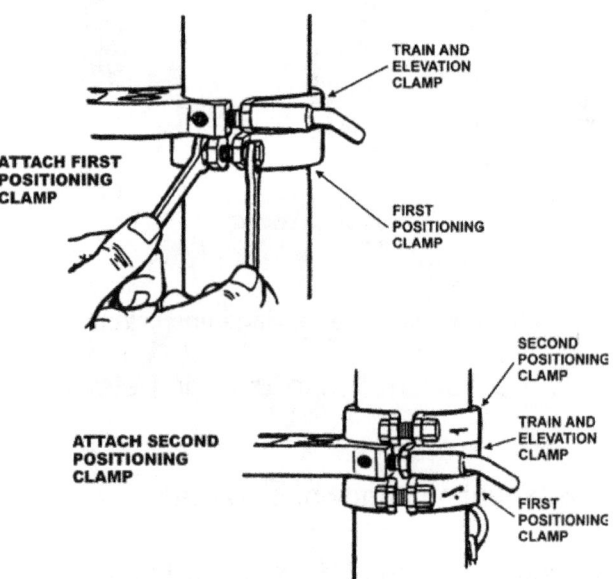

Figure 3-36 Train and elevation middle clamp

(f) Install a support clamp above the middle clamp. To allow free left and right traverse of the carriage and cradle assembly, loosen the train lock handle. To lock in place, tighten the handle.

NOTE- The second or lower set of clamps is not used in this application since the train lock rests on the built-up base of the HMMWV pedestal. This application will also allow for increased elevation. Using two 9/16-inch open-end wrenches, fasten one set of clamps above the middle clamp. Tighten each screw two turns until snug.

(g) Attach the train and elevation assembly to the carriage and cradle assembly by following these procedures:

(1) Pull out the front stow pin to allow the cradle to move.

(2) Pull out the train and elevation assembly's retaining pin.

(3) Ensure the elevating handwheel is set at 250 mils. Position the lock lever to the rear and ensure the traversing knob is on the left.

(4) Turn the traversing knob to center the elevating screw in the yoke.

NOTE: Ensure the elevating handwheel does not get jammed under the lip of the cradle.

(5) Turn the elevating handwheel to align the elevating mechanism holes with the lower rear holes in the cradle.

(6) Insert the retaining pin and rotate to the locked position.

(h) Mount the ammunition can bracket by following these procedures:

(1) Partly unscrew the wing nut on the threaded stud of the bracket mounting assembly. Align the stud with the forward groove in the gun cradle's side plate. Push the bracket mounting assembly up until the heads of the two mounting pins align with the two forward keyholes. Push the heads of the two mounting pins into the keyholes and allow the bracket mounting assembly to slide down. Tighten the wing nut behind the side plate of the cradle (Figure 3-37).

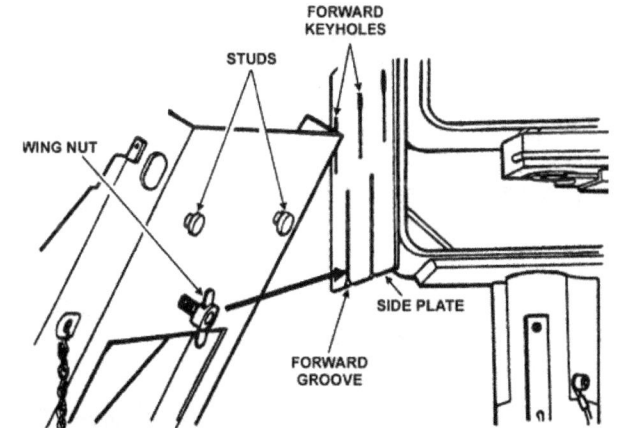

Figure 3-37 Attachment of bracket mounting assembly

(2) Insert the two hooks on the empty case catch bag through the rear holes in the gun cradle. Engage the single front hanger on the catch bag with the hook on the gun cradle (Figure 3-38).

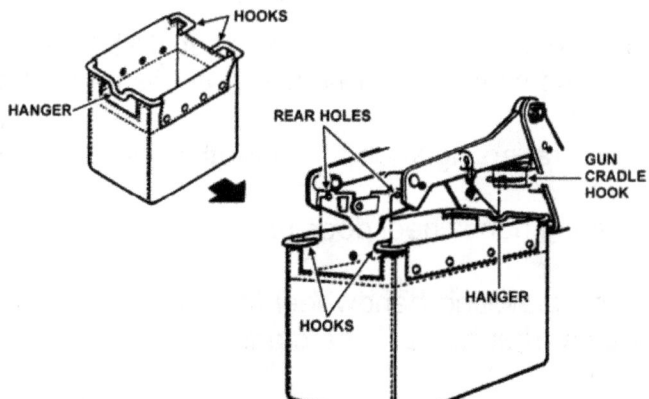

Figure 3-38 Attachment of empty case catch bag

(2) **M66 Ring Mount (2 1/2- to 5-ton cargo trucks).** To mount the MK19 on the M66 ring mount follow these procedures:

    (a) Insert the pintle adapter into the M36A2 ring mount with the M66 ring receptacle.

    (b) Install the gun cradle and mount the MK19.

    (c) Attach the bracket mounting assembly and the empty case catch bag.

(3) **Commander's Cupola (M113 APC).** To mount the MK19 on the commander's cupola follow these procedures:

    (a) Install the pintle adapter and the gun cradle.

    (b) Mount the MK19 and attach the bracket mounting assembly and the empty case catch bag.

    (c) Install the machine gun pintle adapter in the commander's cupola mount by pushing the lock handle down.

    (d) Pull the lock handle up if it does not come up when the pintle is installed.

    (e) Insert the front stow pin to prevent relative movement of the carriage and cradle.

    (f) Insert the carriage pintle into the top of the pintle adapter assembly.

    (g) Press in on the pin's quick-release button and insert the pin.

    (h) Pull upward and twist the carriage and cradle assembly. It should be locked into the pintle adapter, but it should traverse freely left and right.

(i) To remove, reverse the steps.

(4) **The M88 Recovery Vehicle Mount.** To mount the MK19 on the M88 recovery vehicle mount, follow these procedures:

(a) Loosen the traverse locking screw.

(b) Install the machine gun pintle in the machine gun mount.

(c) Insert the front stow pin to prevent movement of the carriage and cradle. Insert the carriage pintle into the top of the pintle adapter assembly.

(d) Press in on the pin's quick-release button and insert the pin.

(e) Pull upward and twist the carriage and cradle assembly. It should be locked into the pintle adapter, but it should traverse freely left and right.

(f) To remove, reverse the steps.

(5) **Weather Cover.** To install the weather cover on the MK19, follow these procedures:

(a) Unzip the zipper on the weather cover.

(b) Pull the weather cover over the barrel, ammunition can, and rear of the MK19.

(c) Zip the zipper to secure.

Loading the MK19

Before loading, the gunner should ensure the MK19 is on S (SAFE) and the bolt is in the forward position.

A. Before loading, use the following procedures:

(1) Attach the feed throat by squeezing the spring-loaded pins on the feed throat.

(2) Insert the feed throat on both sides of the feeder.

(3) Ensure that the feed throat points down.

B. When loading, use the following procedures:

(1) Insert the first round into the feeder (female link first) (Figure 2-39).

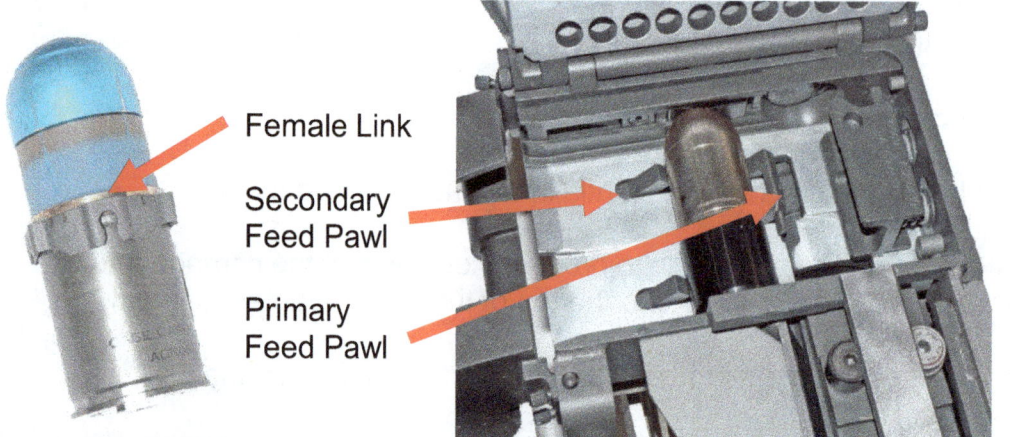

Figure 2-39 Loading of first round (single round shown for explanation)

(2) Push the round across the secondary feed pawl. To move the feed slide to the left, push the secondary drive lever to the right (Figure 2-40).

(3) Close the cover.

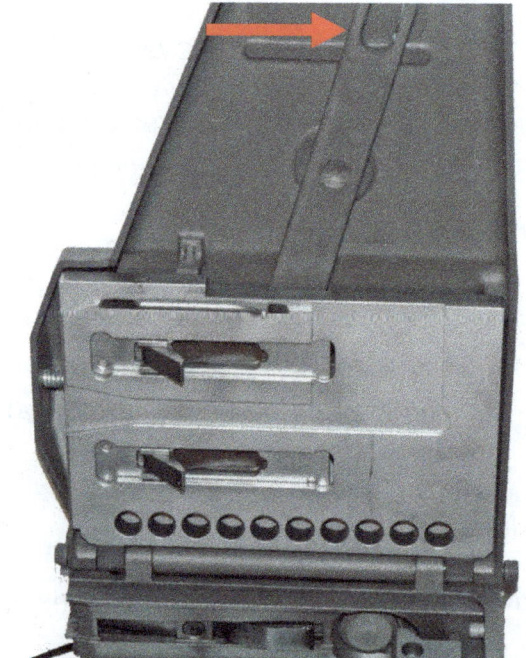

Figure 2-40 Positioning of feed slide assembly

(4) Grasp the charger handles with the palms down.

(5) Press the charger handle locks in.

(6) Rotate the handles down and pull them sharply to the rear.

(7) Return the charger handles forward to their original upright position, after locking the bolt to the rear.

(8) Place the safety switch on F (FIRE) and press the trigger. The bolt slams forward and grasps the first round in the bolt extractors.

(9) Grasp, unlock, and turn charger handles down, and lock the bolt to the rear again.

(10) Ensure the safety switch is on S (SAFE).

(11) Return the charger handles to their original upright position. The MK19 is now ready to fire.

CAUTION- Failure to pull the bolt to the rear completely may result in the misalignment of the M16A2 links on the round, which causes the round to feed improperly.

Firing the MK19

However, to be effective, the gunner must be able to manipulate skillfully the trigger and T&E mechanism; the weapon must be held down and to one side while aiming and adjusting the T&E mechanism. The following steps are simple, but the gunner must remember to estimate the distance to the target, set the sights for distance, manipulate the T&E mechanism, press the trigger, and fire a single round; since the MK19 is a fully automatic weapon, this can only be done by "popping" the trigger once. He must spot the impact of the first round and adjust to the target area. He should begin firing six- to nine-round bursts. This whole process can be done in a matter of seconds, the longest part being the flight time of the round. To fire the weapon:

A. Place the safety on F (FIRE).

B. Ensure the charger handles are in the forward and upright position.

C. Place your hands on the control grips, and your thumb(s) on the trigger.

D. Hold the weapon down and to one side, and check sight picture.

E. Press the trigger to fire.

Zeroing Procedures

Zeroing procedures are crucial for hitting targets at ranges of 600 meters or more. It is strongly recommended that a target at 400 meters be used to zero. The following is the correct way to zero the MK19 to the gunner.

A. Loosen the range plate screw. Move the range plate to the midpoint between the two studs. Tighten the range plate screw. Move the rear sight slide to the meter mark that represents the distance to the target. For example, move to the 400-meter mark to zero on a target known to be 400 meters away. Set the windage knob at the zero index line.

WARNING
Because of the gun's recoil, the first burst is the hardest to control. Ensure that the gun's recoil does not cause the barrel of the weapon to drop and rounds to strike short of the target. Keep it elevated.

B. Align the sights on the base of the target using the T&E mechanism.

C. Fire a single round and spot the impact of the round. If it is on the target, fire another short burst to confirm the zero. If the round is not on target, go on to the next step.

D. To adjust for a round that is not on target, do the following:

(1) If the impact of the round is short or over, adjust the elevation knob. Estimate how short or over the round is. If the round is short, use this estimate to adjust the elevation knob clockwise, which moves the sights up onto the knob counterclockwise to bring the sights down to the target. For example, if the rounds impact 10 mils short, adjust the elevation knob 10 mils up by turning it clockwise. Realign the sights and adjust the gun back on target using the T&E mechanism before the next round is fired.

NOTE: 1. If the adjustment was correct, the second round should be on target. If so, fire the rest of the rounds to confirm the zero. If not, repeat the previous step.

2. If the impacts are not observed, bold adjustments may be necessary.

(2) If the round is to the right or left, adjust the windage knob. Estimate how far to the right or left the sight needs to move to bring the rounds on target. Turn the windage knob clockwise to adjust to the right; turn the windage knob counterclockwise to adjust to the left. For example, if the rounds impact 10 mils to the right, adjust the sight 10 mils to the left by turning the windage knob counterclockwise. Realign and adjust the sights back on target using the T&E mechanism before firing the next round.

(3) Once the zero is completed, align the range plate scale at the exact range of the target used to zero, and tighten it.

E. Point out errors and explain their effect.

F. When the gunner maintains the same sight picture, the type of firing position does not alter the zero.

OPERATION UNDER ADVERSE CONDITIONS

The MK19 is a robust weapon and designed to operate over a wide range of weather conditions, but additional care is required when the temperatures are hot or cold, and the conditions are wet, sandy, or icy.

A. During *hot, wet, or salty air conditions,* follow these procedures:

(1) Inspect the weapon more frequently for signs of rust.

(2) Keep gun as moisture-free as possible.

(3) Field strip, clean, and lubricate more often to preserve metal and prevent rust.

(4) Use a generous second coat of lubrication for extra protection.

B. During *hot, dry, sandy, or dusty conditions,* follow these procedures:

(1) Do not lubricate the entire exposed metal surfaces as this will only collect dust and sand.

(2) Clean the weapon thoroughly and lubricate only the moving components.

(3) Extreme heat dries up lubricant. Clean and lightly lubricate the moving components of the weapon more frequently.

C. During *cold, icy, or snowy conditions,* follow these procedures:

(1) Prior to using cold-weather lubricant, be sure to clean off all existing lubrication. From 0 degrees F to –25 degrees F, use either LSAT, GMD, or LAW. At temperatures –25 degrees F and below, use LAW.

(2) If the weapon "sweats", dry and lube the parts before taking the weapon outdoors and apply a light second coat to provide protection.

(3) Cover weapon if left outside.

(4) If possible, thoroughly clean, dry, and lubricate the weapon in a warm place.

(5) If the weapon is brought indoors, keep it away from direct heat.

(6) Perform functional checks and lubricate daily to help prevent corrosion.

Lubricants to be used
- GMD (Grease, Molybdenum Disulfate)
- LSAT (Lubricant, Semi-Fluid, All-. Temperature)
- LAW (Lubricant, Automatic Weapons)

Classes of Fire
s

Destruction Procedures

Only the commander can direct the destruction of the MK19. There are several ways to destroy it. Methods include destruction by mechanical means, burning, gunfire, demolition or disposal. Use the same methods to destroy equipment. However, ammunition must be handled differently. The best way to destroy ammunition is to fire it. Otherwise, dispose of it by burial, dumping it in a body of water, or using the demolition method.

A. **Mechanical Method.** If possible, use the mechanical method to destroy MK19s and equipment. There are three ways to do this:

(1) Smash them. Using a sledgehammer or some similar heavy tool, damage the MK19s so that they cannot be used.

(2) Bend the MK19s guide rods over the receivers.

(3) Take off (or out) the same part from each of the MK19s. If a different part is taken from each gun, new MK19s may be pieced together.

B. **Burning Method.** To burn equipment or MK19s, use a fuel source that burns hot enough to take the temper from the metal. For example, use jet propulsion fuel (JP-4), oil, or gas. All friendly soldiers in the area are warned before equipment or MK19s are bare burned, because a fire will reveal the positions of friendly forces.

C. **Gunfire Method.** This is the least reliable way to destroy MK19s or equipment. Pile up all of the equipment and MK19s and use MK19s, grenades, or rifles to fire on them. They will scatter so check after shooting to see that they are all destroyed.

D. **Demolition Method.** Use an explosive charge such as composition 4 (C4) or any type of HE round. Place the charges so they will completely destroy all the MK19s and equipment.

E. **Disposal Method.** To dispose of MK19s and equipment, break them down and either scatter the parts into swamps or marshes, or bury them.

WARNING
Ammunition must never be scattered (this may result in a hazard to friendly soldiers), burned (HE and HEDP rounds may explode), or destroyed mechanically.

Section 4

Performance Problems

Stoppages, Malfunctions, Immediate Actions, and Remedial Actions

A stoppage is any interruption in the cycle of operation caused by faulty action of the weapon or ammunition. A malfunction is a failure of the weapon to function properly. Neither defective ammunition nor improper operation of the gun by a crewmember is considered a malfunction of the MK19. This appendix lists the actions to correct common stoppages and malfunctions. For more complete information on troubleshooting common malfunctions and stoppages, refer to TM 9-1010-230-10 Troubleshooting Index.

A stoppage is cleared through immediate or remedial action. Immediate action is the action taken to reduce the stoppage without investigating the cause. The gunner takes remedial action if immediate action does not end the stoppage. Remedial action has three parts: the gunner first unloads and clears the MK19, identifies the problem, and then applies corrective action to fix the problem. If the MK19 still does not fire, or cannot be repaired at the user level, contact the unit armorer.

Immediate Action

Immediate action is different during peacetime and combat.

A. Immediate Action During Peacetime and Training. The gunner does the following immediate action to reduce a stoppage during peacetime.

CAUTION- Both charger handles must be forward and up for firing. If either handle is down, the gun will not fire.

(1) The gunner ensures the safety of other personnel and clears the weapon of ammunition by performing the following steps in sequence:
 (a) Clear the area of personnel.
 (b) Pull bolt to the rear. If the bolt does not go to the rear, go to BOLT JAMMED.
 (c) Catch the live round as it is ejected.
 (d) Push the charging handles forward and up.
 (e) Put the gun on S (SAFE) and check for any bore obstructions.
 (f) If bore is clear, move safety switch from the S (SAFE) to the F (FIRE) position, and attempt to fire.
 (g) If nothing happens, put gun on S (SAFE) and wait 10 seconds.
 (h) Pull the bolt to the rear.
 (i) Catch the live round as it is ejected.
 (j) Open the top cover and clear the ammunition.
 (k) Check bore for any obstructions.

(2) Charge the MK19 in the normal manner and check to see the primary pawls have clicked up behind the cartridge in front of the bolt face and that the secondary pawls have clicked up behind the next round before firing. The feed pawls should click up within the 1-inch of charging handle travel.

(3) If the primary and secondary pawls do not click up within the last 1-inch of charging travel, follow these procedures:
- Turn the MK19 into unit level maintenance.
- Record ammo lot number, type of ammo, number of rounds fired, andserial number of the MK19 and indicate whether ammo is linked with one-piece or two-piece links.

WARNING
1. Do not use combat misfire procedures during peacetime or training. Serious injury can result if precautions are not observed.

2. Do not relink or fire ammunition that has been cycled through the weapon.

Immediate Action During Combat- To correct a misfire during combat, perform the following immediate actions:
(1) Press charger handle locks and rotate charger handles down.
(2) Pull charger handles to the rear until the bolt sears.
(3) Push charger handles forward and rotate charger handles up and lock.
(4) Relay and fire.
(5) Turn in live rounds that cycled through the weapon as instructed by current directives.

Remedial Actions to Clear Stoppages

If the weapon still does not fire, the gunner clears the weapon, identifies the problem, and then takes corrective action to fix or report the problem.

A. **Bad Ammunition-** Bad ammunition can cause a stoppage and is checked first.
(1) **Primer on the Ejected Round is Indented-** Clear the weapon and check to see if the primer is indented. If the primer is indented, it is a bad round and dispose of it as authorized. Reload the weapon and continue with the exercise.

(2) **The Primer Is Not Indented-** Clear the weapon and check to see if the primer is indented. If the primer is not indented, then the firing pin can be bad. Turn the MK19 into unit level maintenance.

(3) **Round on Bolt Face-** Clear the weapon. If the round remains on the bolt face, remove the round and place the weapon on S (SAFE) with the bolt to the rear. Check the primer and see if it is indented. See the aforementioned steps for the corrective action.

B. **Ammunition Jammed in Feeder-** A misfire might occur due to ammunition jammed in feeder. Clear the weapon and put gun on S (SAFE).

WARNING
1. Do not use combat misfire procedures during peacetime or training. Serious injury can result if precautions are not observed.

2. Do not relink or fire ammunition that has been cycled through the weapon.

> (1) **Feed Throat Improperly Attached-** Check for proper attachment of the feed throat. If the feed throat is attached incorrectly, then re-attach it and reload. Try to recharge and fire the weapon. If charging is not possible, go to BOLT JAMMED.
>
> (2) **Rounds Crooked or Not Seated Firmly-** Clear the weapon. If the rounds are crooked or not seated firmly, remove the linked ammunition from feeder. Ensure the link band is even and adjacent to copper band all- around ammo. Reload and continue with the exercise.
>
> (3) **Broken Link-** A broken link can cause the weapon to stop firing. Clear the weapon. If the link is inside the weapon, remove the link. If it is still on the round, then remove the round and dispose it as authorized. Reload and continue with the exercise.
>
> (4) **Link Off Rotating Band-** Clear the weapon. Remove round from belt, dispose of round as authorized. Reload and continue with the exercise.
>
> (5) **Female Link Not First-** A round loaded with the female link not first will cause a stoppage. Clear the weapon. Reload the weapon and ensure that the female link is first.

C. **Bad Firing Pin-** A stoppage might occur due to a bad firing pin or firing pin spring. A possible bad firing pin can be determined while checking for a bad round.

> (1) **Primer on Ejected Round Not Indented-** Clear the weapon. If the primer on the ejected round is not indented, then the firing pin may be bad. Report the defect to the unit armorer.
>
> (2) **Firing Pin Tip Fails to Spring Forward-** Clear the weapon. If the firing pin tip fails to spring forward, then the firing pin spring can be bad. Report the defect to the unit armorer.

D. **Defective Feeder or Feed Slide Assembly-** A misfire might occur due to a defective feeder or feed slide assembly.

CAUTION- Clear feeder of ammunition. Make sure gun is on S (SAFE).

(1) **Broken or Worn Feed Pawls-** Clear the weapon and check to see if the primary and secondary pawls are broken, worn, or without spring action, or if the pin is missing or dislodged. If they are, turn the MK19 into unit level maintenance.

(2) **Badly Worn or Gouged Link Guides-** Clear the weapon and check to see if the guides are worn or gouged. If they are, turn the MK19 into unit level maintenance.

(3) **Binding Feed Slide Assembly-** Clear the weapon. Remove the feed slide assembly and tray. Clean, inspect, and lubricate feed assembly and tray. If the feed slide assembly continues to bind, report the defects to armorer or support maintenance.

E. **Bolt Won't Pick Up the Round-** A misfire might occur because a bolt won't pick up the round.

(1) **Charging Handles are Down-** Clear the weapon. Raise the charging handles before firing. If the weapon still does not fire, report defects to the armorer or support maintenance.

(2) **Dirt-Clogged, Weak, or Damaged Extractors-** Clear the weapon and remove obstruction. Clean, lubricate, and reload weapon. Continue with the exercise.

(3) **Feed Slide Out of Adjustment-** Clear the weapon. The feed slide is out of adjustment if:
- Round fails to feed.
- Round drops.
- Extractors won't pick up round.
- Round stubs on face of chamber.

Report defects to armorer or support maintenance.

F. **Bolt Drops a Round Before Firing-** A stoppage may occur because a bolt drops a round before firing.

(1) **Weak or Damaged Extractors or Bolt Fingers-** Clear the weapon and check for weak or damaged extractors or bolt fingers. Report any defects to the armorer or support maintenance.

(2) **Binding Receiver Rails-** A misfire might occur because of binding receiver rails. Clear the weapon and pull the bolt to the rear without stopping or pausing. Ease it forward (holding onto one charging handle while you press the trigger) and check for binding. Place weapon on S (SAFE) and remove backplate pin. Lift up slightly on the backplate assembly and pull the bolt and backplate assembly to the rear. Remove the chargers. Check the charger rails and receiver rails for burrs. Report defects to armorer or support maintenance.

WARNING
Be sure bolt is forward before removing backplate pin assembly. If not, serious injury could result.

CAUTION- When installing bolt and backplate, ensure cocking lever is in the forward position. Damage to equipment could result if cocking lever is to the rear.

G. **Bad Cocking Lever-** Clear the weapon and remove the bolt and backplate assembly. Examine the cocking lever on the left side of the bolt for wear or damage. Report defects to armorer or support maintenance.

H. **Unknown Cause-** If the MK19 stops firing and the procedures above do not identify and correct the problem, then turn it into the armorer or support maintenance.

Malfunctions, Emergency Actions and Remedial Actions

A malfunction is a failure of the weapon to function properly. Neither defective ammunition nor improper operation of the gun by a crewmember is considered a malfunction of the MK19. The two most common MK19 malfunctions are sluggish action and runaway gun.

CAUTION- Do not attempt to break the ammunition belt; injury could result. Lower one charging handle to stop the gun.

WARNING
1. Before performing any non-firing procedure, ensure the weapon is clear of any ammunition.

2. Ensure all ammunition and non-essential personnel are at least 65 meters to the rear of the weapon.

3. If the bolt jams during firing, do not let the bolt slam forward as the top cover is being opened because a round could fire.

4. Be sure to put bolt in forward position before removing the backplate pin assembly. Serious injury can result if the pin assembly is removed with the bolt to the rear.

5. Be prepared to catch dropped/ejected live round from weapon.

Sluggish or Erratic Firing

Excessive friction from dirt, carbon buildup, lack of lubrication, or burred parts usually causes sluggish or erratic action. Once the gunner realizes that the gun is operating sluggishly or erratically, he should cease-fire and clear the weapon. The two primary corrective actions are cleaning or turning the weapon into the armorer. There are several reasons why a weapon may exhibit sluggish or erratic firing.

A. **Dirty Bore or Chamber-** A dirty bore or firing chamber can cause sluggish or erratic firing. Clear the weapon and clean its bore and chamber. Reload and continue with the exercise.

B. **Recoil Springs or Guide Rods-** Clear the weapon and remove the bolt and backplate assembly from gun. Push against springs to test for weakness. Note bent rods. Report defect to armorer or support maintenance.

C. **Bolt Sear Timing Adjustment-** Clear the weapon and turn it into direct support maintenance.

Runaway Gun

A runaway weapon continues to fire after the trigger has been released. Worn parts or short recoil of the bolt assembly may cause a runaway gun. Consider the amount of ammunition left and the type of MK19 mount used when determining the best way to stop the weapon.

A. **Emergency Action-** This paragraph addresses emergency actions that must be taken to stabilize uncontrolled automatic fire. The following procedures should be taken to control a runaway gun:

(1) If ammunition is not low and the MK19 is used in the free gun mode, keep rounds on target until the all the rounds on the belt have been fired.

(2) If the MK19 is mounted on either the M3 tripod or on a vehicle with the T&E mechanism attached, hold the grip with one hand. At the same time, press the charger handle lock and lower one charger handle. This action interrupts the cycle of operation, causing the MK19 to cease firing. The gunner therefore:

(a) Keeps gun pointed downrange and slightly elevated.
(b) Presses charger handle locks.
(c) Lowers the charging handle(s) so the gun will stop firing.
(d) Places the gun on S (SAFE).

WARNING
Never try to break the ammo belt with your hands. Injury could result. Lower one charger handle to stop gun from firing.

B. Once the gun has stopped firing, clear the weapon and report the condition to the armorer or support maintenance.

Bore obstruction

A bore obstruction is indicated by a muffled sound of round firing, excess smoke out of the chamber, and/or excess debris/gases below the gun.

A. **Emergency Action-** The emergency actions for an obstructed bore are the following:
  (1) Place weapon on S (SAFE).
  (2) Notify range safety officer (during training).
  (3) Depress feed pawls, release ammunition belt, and clear feed.
  (4) Move the ammunition belt and can to a safe area.
  (5) Remove the empty case catch bag.
  (6) Charge gun and hold bolt to rear.

WARNING
Do not relink or fire any ammunition that has been cycled through the weapon.

  (7) Holding the bolt to the rear, insert a cleaning rod through the receiver rail to the top of the shell casing and as close to the face of the bolt as possible.
  (8) Place left hand underneath as close to the round as possible. Raise cleaning rod upward, forcing the round off the bolt face into the hand. Remove round to designated area for explosive ordinance disposal (EOD).

B. **Correcting an Obstructed Bore-** To correct an obstructed bore, follow these procedures:

  (1) Place selector lever on F (FIRE) and ease the bolt forward.

WARNING
Do not relink or fire any ammunition that has been cycled through the weapon.

WARNING
Never try to break the ammo belt with your hands. Injury could result. Lower one charger handle to stop gun from firing.

  (2) Remove the backplate pin bolt, backplate assembly, vertical cam assembly, and primary drive lever.
  (3) Check for any type of obstruction.
  (4) Check and remove any case or round from bolt face.
  (5) Insert bore obstruction detector into bore to check for a live round.
  (6) Remove obstruction per round removal procedures (for exact bore obstruction instructions using the round removal tool, refer to WP 0014 00).

Gun Fires Too Soon

If the weapon fires too soon, or when the trigger is not engaged, the gunner applies emergency action, and the weapon is taken to support maintenance. The gunner must not continue to fire the weapon. The following emergency actions must be taken if a weapon fires too soon:

WARNING
Do not attempt to clear the weapon if the weapon fires too soon. Do not attempt to clear or fire the weapon until it is fixed.

    (1) Cease fire.
    (2) Place weapon on S (SAFE).
    (3) Clear area of personnel and ammunition.
    (4) Notify the range safety officer.
    (5) Check barrel for lodged round using the bore obstruction detector (BOD).
    (6) After proper personnel have cleared weapon, evacuate weapon to support maintenance.

Bolt Jammed

The following actions are taken if the gunner cannot pull the bolt to the rear.

A. **Emergency Action and the Bolt Can Be Pulled to the Rear-** The following emergency actions must be taken if the weapon initially jams, but the bolt can then be pulled to the rear.

WARNING
The following procedures must be performed in sequence to open the top cover. The bolt could spring forward suddenly and fire a round causing severe injury. Be prepared to catch ejected round.

    (1) Put gun on S (SAFE).
    (2) Press charger handle locks and rotate charger handles down.
    (3) Pull charger handles to the rear as far as possible, without stopping or pausing, until bolt locks. Ensure bolt will stay to the rear before releasing charger handles.
    (4) Maintain rearward pressure on charging handles while assistant lifts top cover.
    (5) Insert cleaning rod section through slot in side of receiver. Prepare to the catch ejected, live round.
    (6) Raise cleaning rod to force live round down. Catch live round as it is ejected.
    (7) Remove ammo belt from feeder.
    (8) Reposition ammo belt in feeder.
    (9) Put gun on F (FIRE).
    (10) Ride the bolt forward by grasping one charging handle and depressing the trigger.
    (11) Ensure feed slide assembly is to the left.
    (12) Ensure secondary drive lever is engaged with the feed slide pin. If not, engage forked end with feed slide pin.
    (13) Close top cover gently.

(14) Charge weapon and attempt to fire.
(15) If bolt still jams, repeat first seven steps. Put weapon on S (SAFE), and evacuate to support maintenance.

B. **Gunner's Actions-** The gunner performs the following action once emergency actions are completed:

(1) Clear the jam and make sure there is no bore obstruction.

(2) Charge the MK19 in the normal manner, and check to see if the primary pawls have clicked up behind the cartridge in front of the bolt face and the secondary pawls have clicked up behind the next round before firing. The feed pawls should click up within 1 inch of the charging handle travel.

(3) Check the ammo link to ensure it is even and touches the copper band all around the ammo. If the primary and secondary pawls do not click up within the last 1 inch of the charging handle then:
- Turn MK19 into unit level maintenance.
- Record ammo lot number, type of ammo, number of rounds fired, and serial number of the MK19 and indicate whether ammo is linked with one-piece or two-piece links.

(4) If the MK19 does not require feed slide adjustment and there appears to be no other deficiencies that would prevent the weapon from firing, it should be turned into the armorer or support maintenance.

Short Recoil

A short recoil occurs when the bolt does not fully return to the rear.

WARNING
When firing HE or TP ammunition, the gunner should observe downrange and attempt to determine if the round left the barrel and also should be alert to these three danger signals:
1. **A muffled report from the gun.**
2. **Smoke and debris from the bottom of the receiver.**
3. **Failure of the projectile to leave the muzzle.**

Any of these three symptoms can mean a bore obstruction. Do not attempt to clear a bore obstruction.

A. **Emergency Actions after a Short Recoil-** The gunner does the following actions after a short recoil:

(1) Place weapon on S (SAFE).
(2) Clear area of personnel and ammunition.
(3) Notify range safety officer.

(4) Pull the charger handles to the rear, without stopping or pausing, until the bolt locks. Ensure that the bolt stays to the rear before releasing the charger handles.
(5) Insert cleaning rod section through slot in side of receiver. Prepare to catch the ejected live round.
(6) Raise cleaning rod to force live round down. Catch the live round as it is ejected.
(7) Raise top cover.
(8) Remove ammo belt from feeder.
(9) Check for bore obstruction using bore obstruction detector.
(10) If bore is obstructed, refer to the section above on clearing bore obstructions or refer to WP 0014 00 for round removal procedures.
(11) If there is no obstruction, reposition belt in feeder.
(12) Ensure feed slide assembly is to the left.
(13) Charge weapon and attempt to fire.

If a short recoil occurs again, repeat the first eight steps. Put weapon on S (SAFE) and turn it into support maintenance.

Top Cover Will Not Close

The gunner checks the following so that the top cover can be closed.

A. Improper Position of the Feed Slide Assembly- Move feed slide assembly all the way left. The spring should touch the cover.

B. Bolt is Locked to the Rear- Ride the bolt forward.

C. Misaligned Ammunition- Ensure rounds are straight and firmly seated in the feeder. Ensure links are evenly aligned in the link guide and on rounds. Clean dirt from the feeder.

REFERENCES:
- MCWP 3-15.1: Machine Guns and Machine Gun Gunnery
- FM 23.27 MK19, 40mm Grenade Machine Gun, Mod 3

Appendix A - Ammunition

WARNING- Inspect all cartridges for uniformity, cleanliness, and serviceability. Check all for undented primers, and use only issued ammunition.

M430 HEDP (high-explosive, dual-purpose) Cartridge
The HEDP (high-explosive, dual-purpose) M430 cartridge, joined with M16A2 links, is the standard round for the MK19. The impact-type round penetrates 2 inches of steel armor at 0-degree obliquity and inflicts personnel casualties in the target area. This round is packed in an M548 ammunition container (48 rounds, linked, in each container). It is olive drab with a yellow ogive and yellow markings. It has a PIBD, M549 fuze, and Comp B filler. It arms between 18 to 30 meters and has a casualty radius of 15 meters, figure A-1.

- Identification-Olive drab with yellow-olive and yellow markings
- Fuze-Point initiating, base detonating (PIBD) M549
- Filler-Composition B
- Arming distance-18 to 30 meters
- Kill radius-Approximately 5 meters
- Maximum range-2,200 meters
- Wound radius-Approximately 15 meters
- Maximum effective range-1,500 meters

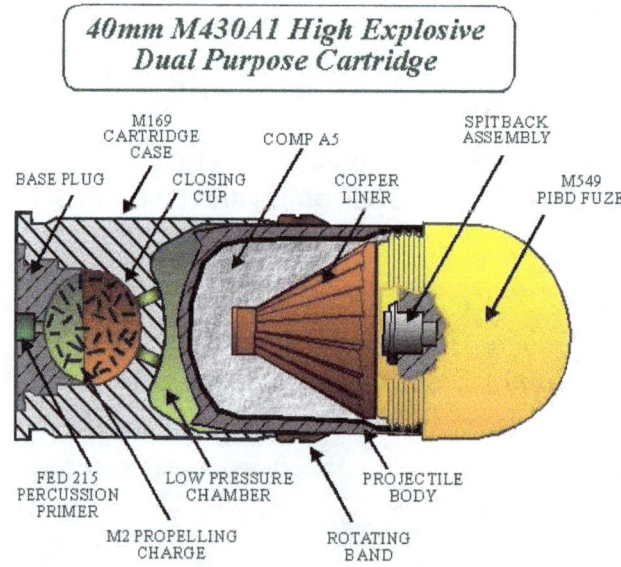

Figure A-1 M430A1 HEDP

M383/M384 40mm HE (high-explosive) Cartridge
The two HE (high-explosive) cartridges inflict personnel casualties in the target area with ground burst effects. Their fillers and body materials differ, although performance traits

are the same. Neither has the armor penetrating ability of the HEDP M430 round. They are both in wooden boxes, 50 rounds to a box.
- HE M383 or M383E1. These rounds are linked with M16A2 links, DODAC B571.
- HE M384. These rounds are linked with M16A2 links, DODAC B470.

The M383 is designed to inflict personnel casualties. It is packed in linked, 48-round belts.
- Fuze-Primer detonating (PD) M533
- Filler-Composition AS
- Arming distance-18 to 36 meters
- Blast radius-15 meters
- Maximum range-2,200 meters

M385 40mm Practice Cartridge

The M385 is an inert round with a propellant charge, figure A-2. The M385 practice rounds are joined with either M16A1 OR M16A2 links, B490. They are packed the same as the HE rounds, in wooden boxes, 50 rounds to a box.

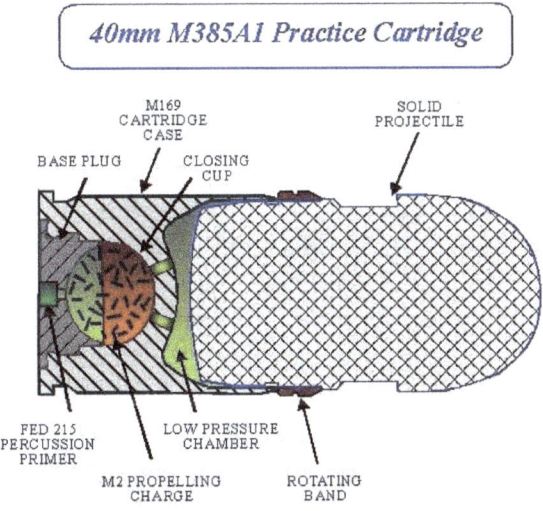

Figure A-2 M385 Practice round

M918 40mm Practice Cartridge

The M918 is a flash-bang round with a propellant charge. The M918 is a training practice cartridge that has the same muzzle velocity of 790 feet per second (fps), signature, and sound as the HE round (DODIC B584).
- Propellant-M2
- Maximum range-2,200 meters
- Maximum effective range-1,500 meters

M922/M922A1 40mm Dummy Cartridge

These rounds are totally inert and are used to check gun functioning and to train gun crews, figure A-3. They are issued only to armorers. The M922 dummy cartridges are joined with M16A2 links. Each MK19 is issued one 10-round belt (DODAC B472), which is packed in an M2A1 metal box.

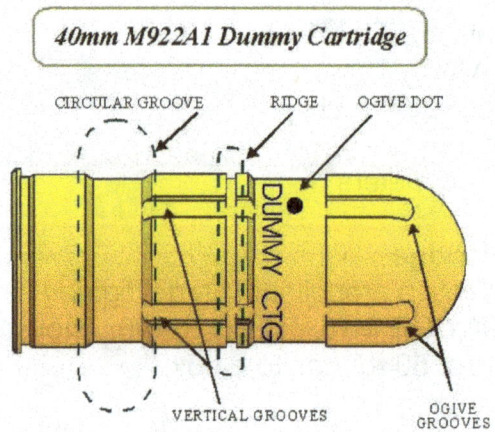

Figure A-3 M922A1 Dummy round

40mm High Velocity Canister Cartridge (HVCC)

The 40mm high Velocity Canister Cartridge (HVCC), fired from the MK19 Grenade Machine Gun (GMG), allows the operator to change radically the use of the MK19 GMG from a stand-off area weapon to a short-range anti-personnel and perimeter defense weapon, figure A-4.

• Type Classified by GD-OTS in April 2001 under a contract managed by the Product Manager Small Arms (PMSA) as part of the Soldier Enhancement Program (SEP)
• Fully functional in the MK19 Grenade Machine Gun (GMG)
• Highly lethal against personnel and provides suppression against protected personnel
• Provides short-range perimeter defense capability for MK19 GMG

Figure A-4 HVCC Flechette Round

Practical Guide to the Operational Use of the **MK19 MOD3 Grenade Machine Gun**

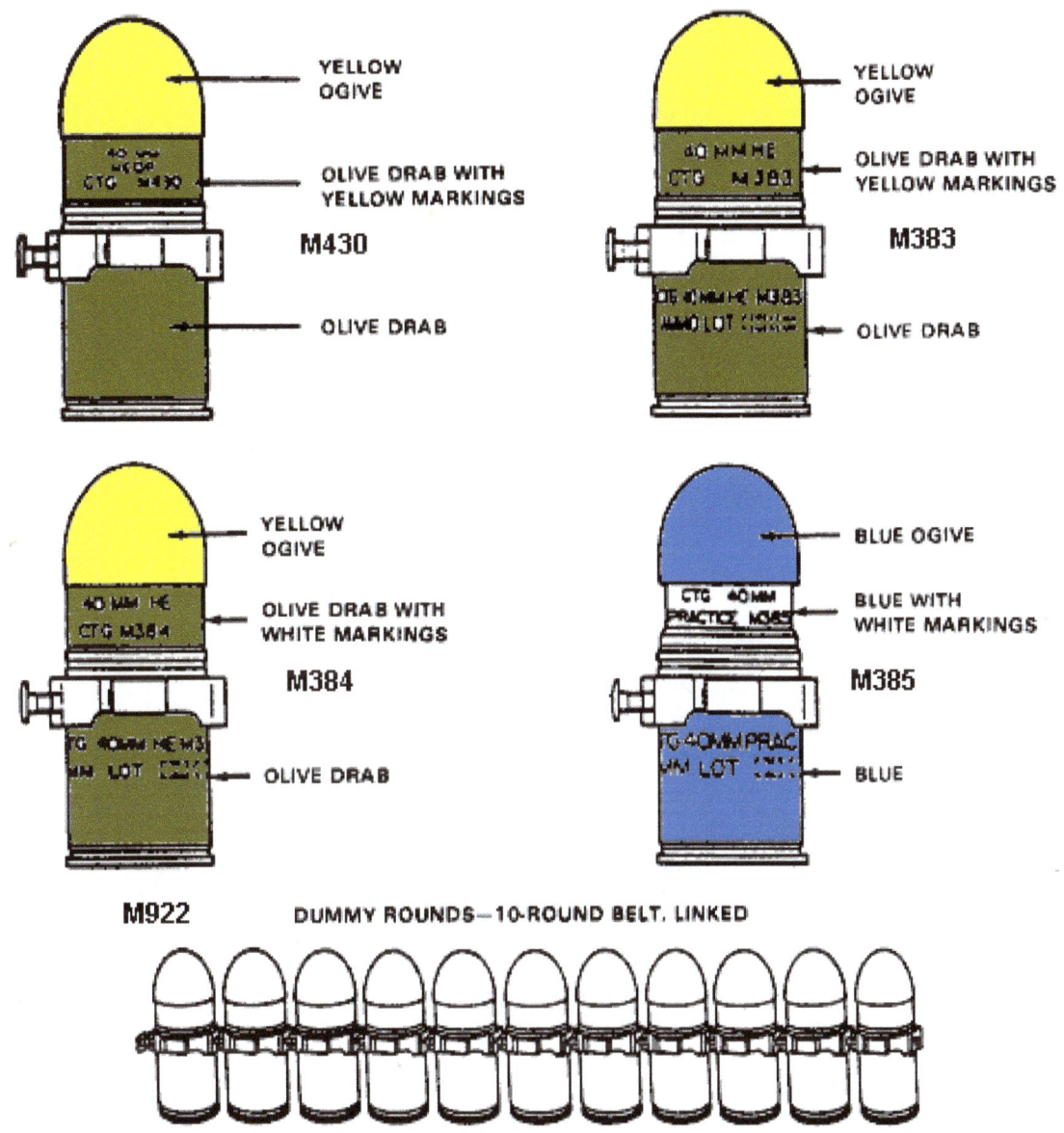

Figure A-5 40 x 53mm marking on cartridges

Ammunition Precautions

A. Ammunition containers should not be opened until you are ready to use them.

B. You should protect the ammunition from mud, dirt, and water. If the ammunition gets dirty or corroded, it must be cleaned before firing.

C. Do not expose ammunition to the direct rays of the sun for long periods of time.

D. Do not oil or grease ammunition, as it will collect dirt.

E. Replace any defective ammunition when you check it prior to firing.

F. Any ammunition marked **"FOR TRAINING PURPOSE ONLY"** is not to be fired over the heads of friendly troops.

www.ingramcontent.com/pod-product-compliance
Lightning Source LLC
Chambersburg PA
CBHW080524110426
42742CB00017B/3221